Name Qasim Riaz
Class 4
Teacher Qari Qasim
Madrasah Ghausia Madrasah

Qamar Islamic Studies Level Four

Second edition, August 2018

Part of the Qamar Islamic Studies series

Published by

Qamar Learning Academy, Bolton, England

admin@qamarislamicstudies.org

Edited by

Mohsin Adam Haveliwala

Cover design by

Maksud Yusuf

Copyright ©2017 Qamar Islamic Studies. The name Qamar and the corresponding logo are trademarks of Qamar Learning Academy. All rights reserved. No part of this publication may be reproduced, stored in a retrieval system, or transmitted in any form or by any means, electronic, mechanical, photocopying, recording or otherwise without the prior permission of the publisher.

Designed and created by Qamar Learning Academy in the UK 🇬🇧

ISBN: 978-1-9997906-3-9

Level Four

QAMAR

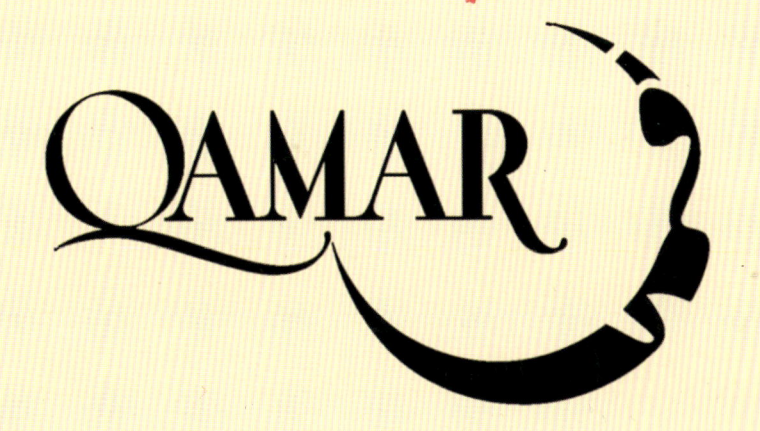

Qamar Learning Academy

Preface

All praise belongs to Allah ﷻ most high, who guided us to Islam, gave us the opportunity to seek His pleasure through serving the faith and strengthened us through His immense generosity.

Let the loftiest of salutations be showered upon our Liege Lord Muhammad ﷺ, his family, companions and all those who follow his way.

Following the initial publication of Level Four in August of 2017, our dearest teachers, students and readers were kind enough to highlight some opportunities for improvement within the book. The second edition of Level four seeks to bring updated lessons to learners with even greater benefit to be attained from this set of critical lessons.

Qamar Academy's aim is to try and enhance the learning experience for children across the UK and we have sought to further our aims through the changes made since the first edition was published. We ask Allah ﷻ to grant us sincerity, accept our meagre efforts and help us to aid young Muslims in their learning journey.

I would like to thank all those who have helped us once again and I look forward to working with the brothers and sisters who will, if Allah wills, help us in the future.

We accept that we will fall short of perfection. If you find any errors in this work, then please write to us on the e-mail address on the inside cover of the book.

We ask Allah ﷻ for success.

Mohsin Adam Haveliwala

August 1st 2018, 18 Zul Qa'dah 1439

The Role of Parents

It is amazing to see the position that Allah ﷻ has granted us in this life. He has made us parents but also guardians of children who will form a part of the future of this world.

Our fate in this world and the next is tied to the fate of our children. As a parent, it is easy to be overwhelmed by the level of responsibility we carry in this regard. There are some simple steps that we can take, as well as things we can think about, in order to ensure that we facilitate a positive learning journey for our children. It is worth reflecting on some of these mentioned below.

1. The eyes and ears of children are the entry points into their souls. Whatever enters their souls from the eyes or ears will have some impact on their spiritual and intellectual wellbeing. It is best to be wary and protect their souls adequately.

2. The most significant teaching relationship children have is with their parents. If they see certain actions and hear certain words from their parents, they will immediately be driven towards accepting them.

3. Good quality learning at home is far more powerful for a child's development than any classroom-based activities.

4. Regularly talking with children about what they have learnt will enhance their learning experience and increase the level of benefit they attain.

5. It is best to allocate a certain time once or twice a week to review the content of a child's learning journey. Only then can we be confident of understanding their progress.

6. Reading to your child regularly is very important for the reinforcement of a learning message.

7. Listen to your child reading regularly.

8. Ask your child to read to you and to tell you the stories that they have learned.

9. Set an expectation with your child each week and map the journey on a wall poster so that they know what to aim for.

10. Rewarding children's achievements will ensure that they enjoy a positive learning experience.

11. Ask Allah ﷻ for success in their learning as all matters are for His pleasure.

Finally, you can ensure that your child's learning is advanced through their everyday life by helping them to complete actions in line with the Qur'aan and Sunnah. Helping them perform wudhu, ghusl, helping them to eat, drink and interact with others in an Islamic manner. This can be further enhanced through sound discipline by limiting time with a TV, computer games, excessive socialisation and music.

We ask Allah ﷻ for success on behalf of our children, ourselves and all people everywhere.

Contents

AQIDAH

Lesson One- The All Forgiving	12
Lesson Two- Messengers Of Allah	18
Lesson Three- Our Prophet Muhammad	24
Lesson Four- Signs of Qiyamah	32
Lesson Five- Major Signs	40
Lesson Six- Death	48
Lesson Seven- Day of Judgement	52
Lesson Eight- Jannah (Paradise)	58
Lesson Nine- Jahannam (Hell)	64

FIQH (HANAFI)

Lesson One-Types of Impurity	70
Lesson Two-Ghusl	76
Lesson Three-Wudhu	80
Lesson Four-Tayammum	88
Lesson Five-Times of Salah	94
Lesson Six-Salah	98
Lesson Seven-Breakers & Makrooh acts of Salah	108
Lesson Eight-Sajdah Al-Sahw	112
Lesson Nine-Prayer of a Masbooq	116
Lesson Ten-The day of Jumu'ah	120
Lesson Eleven-Fasting	122
Lesson Twelve- Hajj (The Pilgrimage)	128

Jalla Jalaluhu. May his glory be exalted.

Sallallahu Alayhi Wa Sallam. Allah bless him and grant him peace.

Alayhis Salaam. Peace be upon him.

Qamar Level 4

SEERAH & SHAMAIL

Revision Timeline	134
Lesson One-Quraysh meet at Dar Al-Nadwah	136
Lesson Two-The Hijrah	142
Lesson Three-Arrival in Al-Madinah	148
Lesson Four- Building of the Masjid	156
Lesson Five-The cusp of war	164
Lesson Six-Battle of Uhud	174
Lesson Seven-Battle of Al-Ahzaab	188
Lesson Eight-Rasoolullah's ﷺ blessed lineage	198
Lesson Nine-The beauty of his ﷺ form	200

AKHLAQ

Lesson One-Dhikr (Remembrance) of Allah ﷻ	206
Lesson Two-Kindness to parents	210
Lesson Three-Backbiting	214
Lesson Four-Jealousy	218
Lesson Five-Pride	220
Lesson Six-Visiting the sick	222
Lesson Seven-Halal and Haraam foods	224

Radi Allahu Anhu. May Allah be pleased with him.

Radi Allahu Anha. May Allah be pleased with her.

Radi Allahu Anhuma. May Allah be pleased with them both.

THE SUPPLICATION FOR SEEKING KNOWLEDGE

بِسْمِ اللهِ الرَّحْمٰنِ الرَّحِيْمِ

اَلْحَمْدُ لِلّٰهِ رَبِّ الْعَالَمِيْنَ

وَصَلَّى اللهُ عَلَى سَيِّدِنَا مُحَمَّدٍ وَّعَلَى آلِهِ وَصَحْبِهٖ أَجْمَعِيْنَ

نَوَيْتُ التَّعَلُّمَ وَالتَّعْلِيْمَ وَالتَّذَكُّرَ وَالتَّذْكِيْرَ وَالنَّفْعَ وَالْاِنْتِفَاءَ وَالْاِفَادَةَ وَالْاِسْتِفَادَةَ وَالْحَثَّ عَلَى التَّمَسُّكِ بِكِتَابِ اللهِ وَسُنَّةِ رَسُوْلِهٖ وَالدُّعَاءِ إِلَى الْهُدَى وَالدَّلَالَةَ عَلَى الْخَيْرِ وَابْتِغَاءَ وَجْهِ اللهِ وَمَرْضَاتِهٖ وَقُرْبِهٖ وَثَوَابِهٖ سُبْحَانَهٗ وَتَعَالَى

In the name of Allah ﷻ, the Entirely Merciful, the Especially Merciful

All praise to Allah ﷻ, Lord of the Worlds

And salutations and greetings upon our master Muhammad ﷺ and upon his family and companions

I intend to study and teach, take and give a reminder, take and give benefit, take and give advantage, to encourage the holding fast to the book of Allah ﷻ and the way of His Messenger ﷺ, and calling to guidance and directing towards good, hoping for the countenance of Allah ﷻ and His pleasure, proximity and reward, transcendent is He.

Qamar Learning Academy

اَلعَقِيدَة

What's in this section?

THE ALL FORGIVING
- The one who responds
- The most merciful

MESSENGERS OF ALLAH ﷻ
- The characteristics of Prophets عليهم السلام

OUR PROPHET MUHAMMAD ﷺ

SIGNS OF QIYAMAH
- Major signs
- Appearance of Dajjal

MAJOR SIGNS
- Coming of Sayyiduna Isa
- Yajooj and Majooj
- The Beast

DEATH

DAY OF JUDGEMENT
- Al-Meezan (The scale)

JANNAH (PARADISE)
- Actions that will take us into Jannah

JAHANNAM (HELL)

AQIDAH

LESSON ONE - THE ALL FORGIVING

Al-Ghaffar means the all-forgiving. Allah ﷻ forgives all major and minor sins we commit when we repent to Him sincerely. Even if our sins are enough to fill the entire world, they will be forgiven when we repent to Allah ﷻ.

> Allah ﷻ says "Yet I am all-forgiving to the one who repents and believes and does good works and remains upon guidance."
>
> وَإِنِّي لَغَفَّارٌ لِّمَن تَابَ وَآمَنَ وَعَمِلَ صَالِحًا ثُمَّ اهْتَدَىٰ
>
> Surah Taha, Ayah No: 82

Our Beloved Prophet Muhammad ﷺ says, "Allah ﷻ proclaims "Oh son of Adam, as long as you call me and keep hope in me, I will forgive all that you have done and I don't bother (how much).'" (Al-Tirmidhi).

This hadith teaches us how much Allah ﷻ loves to forgive. Allah's ﷻ mercy and forgiveness is immense. If Allah ﷻ wills, He will forgive a person's sins no matter how great they may be.

Even Sayyiduna Rasoolullah ﷺ, who had no sins, would turn to Allah ﷻ and seek forgiveness seventy times a day. In this way, he taught us about the importance of seeking Allah's ﷻ forgiveness.

We must stay away from committing sins and if we do commit a sin, we must turn to Allah ﷻ immediately and seek His forgiveness.

THE ONE WHO RESPONDS

المجيب

Allah ﷻ is with us and answers our Duaa (supplication). He loves those who ask from him. He helps us when we are in trouble and He makes things easy for us. When we are ill, He is the one who cures us. When we are in need, He is the one who fulfils our needs. When we are hungry, He is the one who provides food for us.

Sayyiduna Abu Hurairah ﷺ reported that the Prophet ﷺ said, *"Our Lord (Allah's ﷻ mercy) descends every night to the heaven of this world when a third of the night remains and says: "(Is there anyone) who supplicates to Me so that I may accept his supplication? (Is there anyone) who asks of Me so that I may give to him? (Is there anyone) who asks for my forgiveness so that I may forgive him?""*

Our Prophet ﷺ was asked which Duaa is most acknowledged by Allah ﷻ. He ﷺ replied *"The Duaa during the last part of the night and the Duaa after the obligatory prayers (Fardh Salah)"*.

Our Prophet ﷺ said *"There are three Duaas which are not rejected by Allah ﷻ. They are:*
1) *The Duaa of a parent for their child.*
2) *The Duaa of the one who is fasting.*
3) *The Duaa of a traveller.*

THE MOST MERCIFUL

Allah is most kind and merciful to everything in creation. The mercy of Allah is given to the believers and non-believers.

We must ask for Allah's mercy and grace. We must also be merciful to all His creation. Our Prophet said *"Those who are merciful will be shown mercy by the Most Merciful. Be merciful to those on the earth and the One in the heavens will have mercy upon you."* (Meaning the one whose dominion is in the heavens) (Al-Tirmidhi)

Sayyiduna Abu Hurairah reported that Rasoolullah said, "A man suffered from thirst while he was walking on a journey. When he found a well, he climbed down into it and drank from it. Then he came out and saw a dog lolling its tongue from thirst and licking the ground. The man said, "This dog has suffered thirst just as I have suffered from it." He climbed down into the well, filled his shoe with water, and caught it in his mouth as he climbed up. Then he gave the dog a drink. Allah appreciated this deed, so He forgave him." (Al-Bukhari)

It is important that we show kindness to every creature, even animals, because Allah is pleased with such kindness.

EXERCISE ONE

MATCH THE NAMES OF ALLAH ﷻ WITH THEIR CORRECT MEANINGS AND ANSWER THE QUESTIONS BELOW.

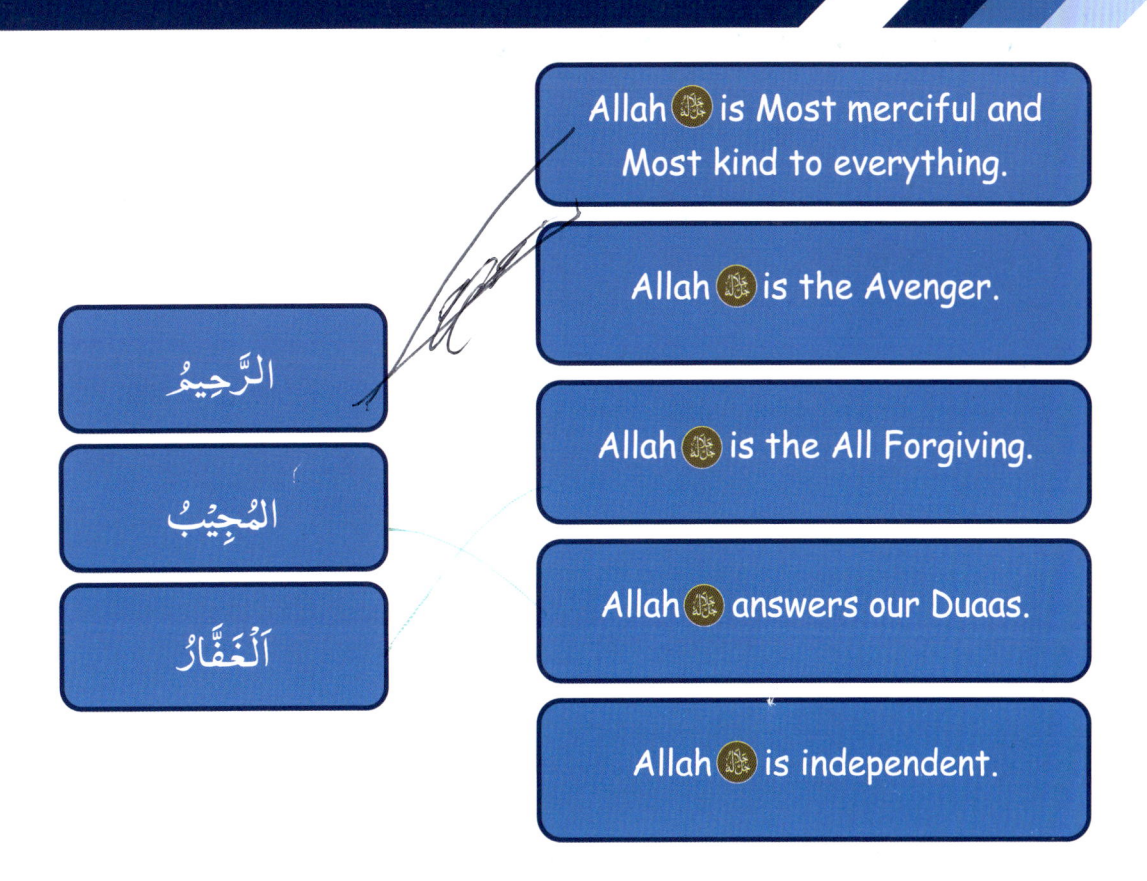

اَلرَّحِيمُ

الْمُجِيبُ

اَلْغَفَّارُ

- Allah ﷻ is Most merciful and Most kind to everything.
- Allah ﷻ is the Avenger.
- Allah ﷻ is the All Forgiving.
- Allah ﷻ answers our Duaas.
- Allah ﷻ is independent.

2. A Muslim should always try to avoid committing a sin. If, however, a person does commit a sin, what should they do?

They must turn to Allah immediatly and seek his forgivness

3. How did Allah show his mercy to the man who helped the thirsty dog?

He forgived him

4. Which Duaas are not rejected by Allah?

- The dua of your fasting
- The dua of traveling
- The dua of a parent to the child

5. Why should we make Duaa to Allah?

Because he will fulfil our needs and will ... us when we are ill

6. Choose one name of Allah ﷻ which is not mentioned in this lesson. Using your own research, design a poster and present your findings to your teacher and friends.

LESSON TWO - MESSENGERS OF ALLAH عليهم السلام

Key Terms

Rasool (Messenger) – A special man who has been given a Shariah from Allah ﷻ and has been ordered to preach it.

Nabi (Prophet) – A special man who has been chosen by Allah ﷻ and ordered to preach the Shariah given to a Rasool.

The first Prophet sent by Allah ﷻ is Sayyiduna Adam عليه السلام and the final Prophet is our beloved Prophet Muhammad ﷺ.

Many Prophets and Messengers عليهم السلام came to different parts of this world. Approximately 124,000 Prophets عليهم السلام were sent to mankind but the exact number is known only to Allah ﷻ and our Prophet Muhammad ﷺ.

We must believe in all Messengers and Prophets عليهم السلام from Sayyiduna Adam عليه السلام to our Prophet Muhammad ﷺ. A person who rejects a single Prophet cannot be called a Muslim.

The characteristics of Prophets ﷺ

Truthfulness: Prophets ﷺ always speak the truth. If they could lie, then people would have no way of knowing whether the Message of Islam they teach is true or not.

Intelligence: All Prophets ﷺ have the highest intelligence and wisdom so that they can answer objections from the people.

Sinless: Prophets ﷺ are protected from sin by Allah ﷻ. They are completely obedient to Allah ﷻ. We have been ordered to follow the footsteps of the Prophets ﷺ and if they had been disobedient then it would have been permissible for us to be disobedient to Allah ﷻ as well.

Beauty: All Prophets ﷺ are beautiful. No Prophet ﷺ was ever sent with a weakness in their body such as blindness. The most beautiful of all creation is Our Beloved Prophet Muhammad ﷺ.

Spread Allah's ﷻ Message: Prophets ﷺ always communicate Allah's ﷻ message as they are commanded. They never add or withhold anything.

Prophets are the best of all Allah's ﷻ creation. The greatest prophet is our Prophet Muhammad ﷺ. Followed by:

- Sayyiduna Ibrahim عليه السلام
- Sayyiduna Musa عليه السلام
- Sayyiduna Isa عليه السلام
- Sayyiduna Nuh عليه السلام

They are the highest ranked Prophets and are referred to as Arch Messengers (أُولُو العَزْمِ). This term means that they are the most superior from amongst the Prophets and Messengers عليهم السلام

To respect all the Messengers and Prophets عليهم السلام is Fardh. The slightest disrespect of any Prophet leads one to Kufr (disbelief).

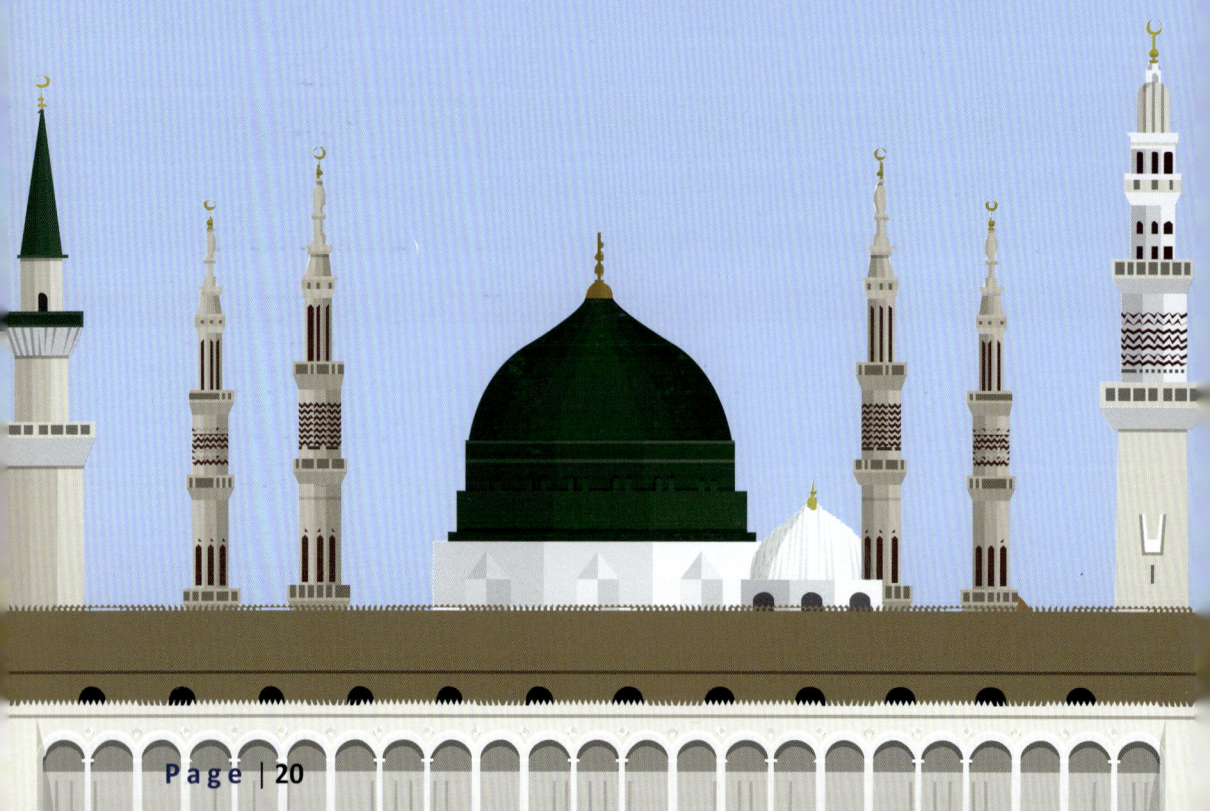

EXERCISE TWO

TICK TRUE OR FALSE FOR EACH OF THE STATEMENTS BELOW.

	True	False
1. As Muslims we believe that all Messengers ﷺ are Male.	✓	
2. Rejecting any Prophet or Messenger ﷺ is fine.		✓
3. Prophets ﷺ are all beautiful but can sometimes have some weaknesses in their bodies.		✓
4. Prophets ﷺ cannot commit any sin.	✓	

Answer the Questions Below

1. List three characteristics of a Prophet ﷺ and explain what each of them means.

_____
_____
_____
_____
_____
_____
_____
_____

2. Why should we follow a Messenger ﷺ?

_____
_____
_____
_____
_____
_____
_____
_____
_____
_____

3. Why did Allah ﷻ protect Prophets عليهم السلام from sin? Explain your answer using examples.

_____
_____
_____
_____
_____
_____
_____
_____
_____
_____
_____
_____

Allah's Messenger ﷺ said,

"Both in this world and in the Hereafter, I am the nearest of all the people to Jesus, the son of Mary. The prophets are paternal brothers; their mothers are different, but their religion is one."

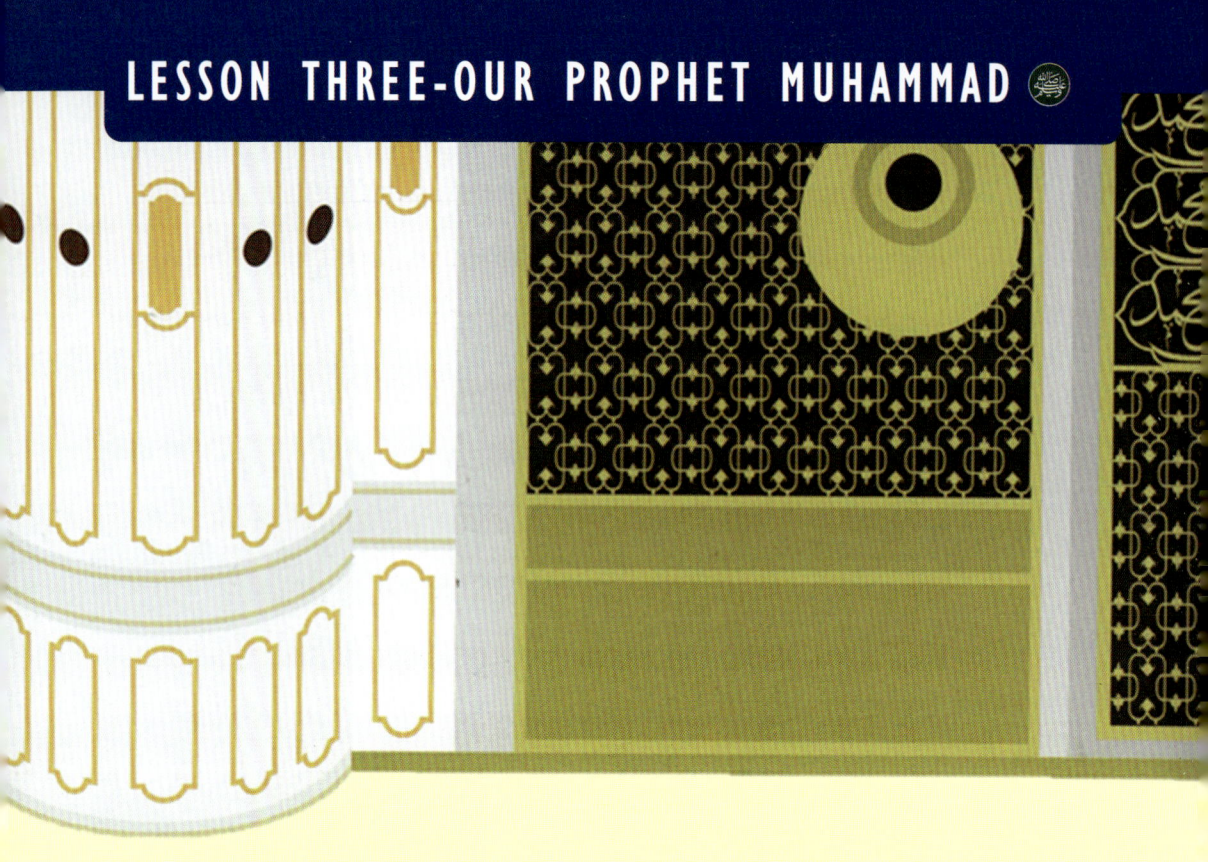

LESSON THREE-OUR PROPHET MUHAMMAD ﷺ

Our Prophet Muhammad ﷺ is the greatest and the most exalted of Allah's ﷻ creation. He is Khatam Al-Nabiyyeen meaning he is the last of all prophets and messengers ﷺ. No new Prophet will come after Him ﷺ and there will be no new book. Anyone who claims to be a Prophet ﷺ or believes in someone who claims to be a Prophet ﷺ after the final messenger ﷺ will no longer be a Muslim.

Our Prophet ﷺ is a mercy for the entire creation of Allah ﷻ. However, He is most merciful upon believers. Allah ﷻ says in the Qur'aan regarding the Prophet ﷺ *"We did not send you but as a mercy to all of the worlds"*. Our Prophet ﷺ would never take revenge for personal matters but would rather show kindness and care for people even if they upset him.

Allah has commanded us to believe in the Prophet.

فَآمِنُوا بِاللَّهِ وَرَسُولِهِ وَالنُّورِ الَّذِي أَنزَلْنَا وَاللَّهُ بِمَا تَعْمَلُونَ خَبِيرٌ

"Believe in Allah and His Messenger and the Qur'aan which We have sent down. And Allah is Acquainted with what you do."

Surah Taghabun:, Ayah No: 8

Allah says in the Qur'aan:

"If your fathers, your sons, your brothers, your spouses, your families, the wealth you own, the trade whose decline you fear and the homes you enjoy are more beloved to you than Allah and his Messenger and striving in His cause, then wait until Allah brings his command to pass; Allah guides not the wicked."

Surah Al-Tawbah: 9, Ayah No: 24

The obligation to love Our Prophet ﷺ

Love for Our Prophet ﷺ is love for Allah ﷻ. Our Prophet ﷺ is the most beloved of all creation to Allah ﷻ. This is one of the most important reasons for us to love him. Let's look at some of the things that show how much Allah ﷻ loves Our Prophet ﷺ Allah ﷻ has made it Fardh upon all Muslims to love the Prophet ﷺ more than their fathers, children, spouses, families and wealth.

Allah ﷻ has ordered us in the Qur'aan to respect and honour our Prophet Muhammad ﷺ. To honour and respect our Prophet Muhammad ﷺ is an essential part of our Imaan (Faith). We already know that Our Prophet ﷺ is the greatest of all creation and He is a Messenger for both man and Jinn.

Our Prophet Muhammad ﷺ will be the leader of all humans on the Day of Judgement. Sayyiduna Abu Hurairah ؓ narrates that Our Prophet ﷺ said *"I will be the master of the sons of Adam on the Day of Judgement and I am not boasting. In my hand will be a banner of praise and I am not boasting. There will be no Prophet that day, Adam or anyone else, but he will be beneath my banner. I am the first one for whom the earth will be split open and I am not boasting."*

On the Day of Judgement Allah ﷻ will grant Our Prophet ﷺ Al-Maqaam Al-Mahmood (the praised station) which is the position of intercession. Everyone will be gathered in one arena and none shall speak except by the permission of Allah ﷻ. No human being will dare to talk to Allah ﷻ but Our Prophet ﷺ will step forward and intercede for his followers to save them from entering the hellfire.

Our Prophet ﷺ will also be the first to enter Jannah.

Allah ﷻ has granted Our Prophet ﷺ a lake-fountain which is known as Al-Kawthar. It is whiter than milk and sweeter than honey.

Allah ﷻ gave numerous miracles to His Prophets عليهم السلام but the greatest miracle was given to Our Prophet Muhammad ﷺ and it is the Qur'aan. No Prophet or Messenger was given a miracle as great as the Qur'aan.

Allah also granted Our Prophet ﷺ the greatest honour of seeing Allah ﷻ which no other Prophet or Messenger عليهم السلام was granted before him.

The obligation to obey him ﷺ

Allah ﷻ commands us to obey Our Prophet ﷺ in the Qur'aan

يَـٰٓأَيُّهَا ٱلَّذِينَ ءَامَنُوٓا۟ أَطِيعُوا۟ ٱللَّهَ وَرَسُولَهُۥ وَلَا تَوَلَّوْا۟ عَنْهُ وَأَنتُمْ تَسْمَعُونَ

"O you who believe, obey Allah and His Messenger and do not turn away from Him while you hear His order"

Surah Al-Anfaal, Ayah No: 20

Believing in Our Prophet ﷺ means that we must obey Him. Allah made obeying Our Prophet Muhammad ﷺ part of obeying Him ﷻ. Obeying Sayyiduna Rasoolullah ﷺ means to cling to His beautiful Sunnah.

We can never forget the immense sacrifices made by Rasoolullah ﷺ so that we would receive the message of Islam. Rasoolullah ﷺ is always concerned about his Ummah.

When Allah ﷻ granted Our Prophet ﷺ fifty obligatory prayers, Our Prophet ﷺ was so concerned about how difficult it would be for us that He kept returning to Allah ﷻ until it was reduced to just five prayers a day.

When Sayyiduna Rasoolullah ﷺ was preaching the message of Islam in Makkah Al-Mukarramah, He suffered great pain in order to convey the message of Islam. At one point, he even travelled to a place called Taif where he was struck by stones until his sandals were full of blood, yet when Allah ﷻ gave him the choice to destroy the people of Taif, He chose to spare them.

Given everything we have mentioned in this lesson, our love for Allah's ﷻ greatest Messenger ﷺ can only grow. We must always try our best to obey Sayyiduna Rasoolullah ﷺ.

One of the greatest ways in which we can show our love for Sayyiduna Rasoolullah ﷺ is by sending blessings and salutations on him. In this way, we venerate Allah's ﷻ most beloved by asking Allah ﷻ to honour Our Prophet ﷺ with his special mercy, blessings and greetings.

Even if we were to spend all our free time reciting Salawaat upon Rasoolullah ﷺ it would not be enough for us to show gratitude to Allah ﷻ for making us one from His Ummah.

Sayyiduna Ubayy Ibn Ka'b ؓ once said to Rasoolullah ﷺ "I make the intention now that I shall set aside all the time of Duaa for Salat upon you."

Rasoolullah ﷺ replied "In that case all your worries shall be removed and your sins shall be forgiven."

EXERCISE THREE

ANSWER THE QUESTIONS BELOW.

1. What is the meaning of Khatamun Nabiyyeen?
   Last of all Prophet and messenger

2. What is the Islamic law for someone who believes that another Prophet will come after Our Prophet Muhammad ﷺ?
   there leafalt wont be a muslim any more and disbleiver

3. Who is Our Prophet Muhammad ﷺ most merciful with?
   believers

4. Why is it important to love Our Prophet Muhammad ﷺ?

6. Find and outline an example of how the companions honoured and respected Our Prophet Muhammad ﷺ. Mention what you have learned from the example.

قُلْ إِن كُنتُمْ تُحِبُّونَ اللَّهَ فَاتَّبِعُونِي يُحْبِبْكُمُ اللَّهُ وَيَغْفِرْ لَكُمْ ذُنُوبَكُمْ وَاللَّهُ غَفُورٌ رَحِيمٌ

Say, [O Muhammad], "If you should love Allah, then follow me, [so] Allah will love you and forgive you your sins. And Allah is Forgiving and Merciful."

LESSON FOUR-SIGNS OF QIYAMAH

This world is temporary and one day it will be destroyed at a time which is only known to Allah ﷻ. However, our Prophet Muhammad ﷺ has informed us about certain signs that will show that the Day of Judgement is close.

Sayyiduna Rasoolullah ﷺ conveyed the knowledge of the Day of Judgement and the signs that will be seen before it to his blessed companions. These signs will be of 2 types; minor and major. The minor signs will appear first followed by the major signs. The major signs will be extraordinary and strange, the appearance of which will mean that the last day is near. You will notice that some of these signs are already apparent.

Minor Signs

- **Music will become very common:** We can see today that every house has TVs and other devices playing Music.
- **The consumption of alcohol will become widespread:** Alcohol is strictly forbidden in Islam so we need to stay away from both alcohol and the places where it is consumed. Alcohol ruins the lives of millions all over the world and has a negative effect on their families and friends.
- **Children will disrespect their parents:** Our parents sacrifice so much for us, however sometimes they are ignored and forgotten especially as children begin to grow older. Our parents deserve to be honoured always. Even if they say something we don't like, we must still respect and love them.

- **Knowledge will be taken away:** The scholars of Islam will leave this world and there will be very few learned scholars.
- **People will lose respect for the house of Allah ﷻ:** They will talk loudly and will shout in the Mosques.
- **Time will pass by very quickly:** A year will pass like a month, a month like a week, a week like a day and a day will pass by as something burns very quickly as soon as it catches fire.
- **There will be an increase in ignorance**: Many Muslims today do not know the basics of their religion.
- **Killing will become more common**: There will be people who will think that the lives of other people are not important. Protecting the life and property of people is very important in Islam. Islam teaches us to protect all and harm none. This includes Humans, animals and all kinds of life. All over the world today, crimes committed using weapons such as guns and knives are increasing. So many innocent people are losing their lives because of these acts of violence.

> مَن قَتَلَ نَفْسًا بِغَيْرِ نَفْسٍ أَوْ فَسَادٍ فِي الْأَرْضِ فَكَأَنَّمَا قَتَلَ النَّاسَ جَمِيعًا
> وَمَنْ أَحْيَاهَا فَكَأَنَّمَا أَحْيَا النَّاسَ جَمِيعًا
>
> "Whoever kills a person [unjustly] it is as though he has killed all mankind. And whoever saves a life, it is as though he had saved all mankind."
>
> Surah Al-Maaidah, Ayah No: 32

- Earthquakes will increase.
- An increase in diseases that were unknown in previous times.
- Wild animals will be able to talk to humans.

MAJOR SIGNS

One major sign of the Day of Judgement is the appearance of Imaam Mahdi ﷺ.

Before his arrival, there will be a lot of corruption and injustice. Muslims will be disunited and weak. Allah ﷻ will then send Imaam Mahdi ﷺ as the leader of the Muslims.

His name will be Muhammad. His father's name will be Abdullah and his title will be 'Al Mahdi' meaning the guided one. He will be a direct descendant of our Prophet Muhammad ﷺ.

Imaam Mahdi ﷺ will reside in Al-Madinah Al-Munawwarah, however at the age of 40, he will leave his residence in Al-Madinah Al-Munawwarah and migrate to Al-Makkah Al-Mukarramah. There, people will approach him in Al-Haram near the Holy Ka'ba and will choose him as their leader.

Imaam Mahdi ﷺ will travel towards the city of Damascus, in Syria. He will fight many battles against the disbelievers. Allah ﷻ will grant him victory over his enemies.

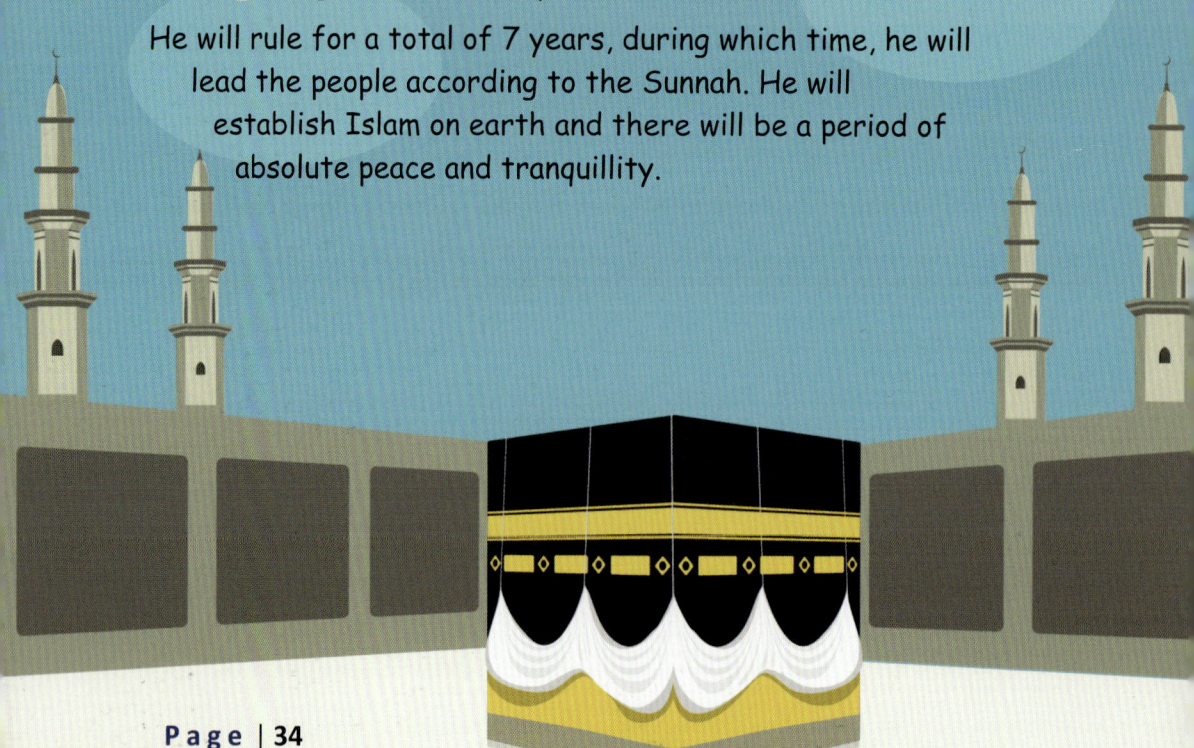

He will rule for a total of 7 years, during which time, he will lead the people according to the Sunnah. He will establish Islam on earth and there will be a period of absolute peace and tranquillity.

APPEARANCE OF DAJJAL

Another major sign of the Day of Judgement is the appearance of Dajjal (The Anti-Christ).
Our Prophet Muhammad ﷺ has described Dajjal with a lot of detail so that we may recognise him if we were to see him.

Dajjal will have curly hair, he will be blind in the right eye.

The Prophet of Allah ﷺ said, *"There is no fitnah (evil) from the time of Adam up to the Final Hour greater than the fitnah (evil) of Dajjal."*

He will appear during the time of Imaam Mahdi ﷺ and will emerge from a place presently known as Isfahan. He will travel the entire world in 40 days. The first day of these 40 days will be like a year, the second like a month, the third like a week and the rest like normal days.

Dajjal's evil and corruption will be very strong, wherever he goes, he will have with him a garden and a huge fire. He will refer to his garden as Paradise and his fire as Hell. In reality, his garden will be the fire of hell and his fire will be the garden of Paradise. Whoever enters his paradise will realise it is hell and whoever enters his hell will find that it is Paradise.

Dajjal will claim to be God. He will order the sky to rain for those who believe in him and will order the earth to produce its fruits so that they and their animals will eat from it. However, those people who reject Dajjal will suffer from a lack of food and water.

Dajjal will try to enter Makkah Al-Mukarramah and Al-Madinah Al-Munawwarah but the Angels of Allah ﷻ will turn him away from these two holy cities. After travelling the entire world, Dajjal will reach Syria.

The coming of Sayyiduna Isa

Sayyiduna Isa (Jesus) ﷺ will descend from the skies placing his hands on the wings of two angels on the Eastern Minaret of the Umayyad Masjid in Damascus. During this moment, Imam Mahdi ﷺ will be about to lead people in the Fajr prayer. The next morning, Sayyiduna Isa ﷺ will advance towards Dajjal with a spear in his hands as the Muslim army attacks the army of Dajjal.

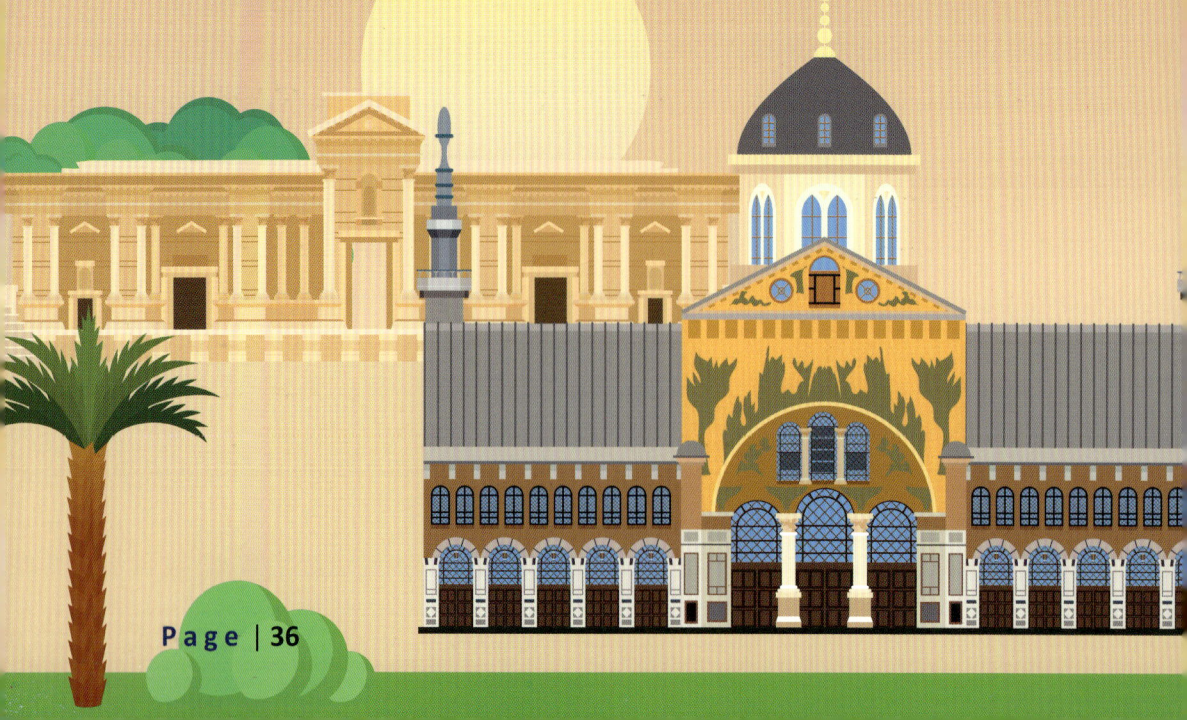

EXERCISE FOUR

ANSWER THE QUESTIONS BELOW.

1. Explain the difference between the minor and major signs before the Day of Judgement.

_____
_____
_____
_____

2. List five signs of the Day of Judgement. Show which ones are major and which ones are minor.

_____
_____
_____
_____
_____
_____

3. Write about one of the signs that you see in the world around you today.

_____
_____
_____
_____
_____
_____

4. Explain how children sometimes disrespect their parents. What should they do instead?

_____
_____
_____
_____
_____
_____

5. Why is it important to protect all kinds of life?

_____
_____
_____
_____
_____
_____
_____
_____
_____
_____
_____

لاَ يَصْبِرُ عَلَى لأْوَاءِ الْمَدِينَةِ وَشِدَّتِهَا أَحَدٌ إِلاَّ كُنْتُ لَهُ شَهِيدًا أَوْ شَفِيعًا يَوْمَ الْقِيَامَةِ

"No one is patient with the difficulties and hardships of Al-Madinah, except that I am an intercessor, or a witness for him on the Day of Judgement."

Sahih Muslim

LESSON FIVE - MAJOR SIGNS: THE COMING OF SAYYIDUNA ISA ﷺ

The coming of Sayyiduna Isa ﷺ is a major sign of the Day of Judgement. Sayyiduna Isa ﷺ was not killed nor did he die but Allah ﷻ raised him to the heavens. Allah ﷻ will send him back into this world before the Day of Judgement.

Our Prophet ﷺ mentioned "*During the Me'raj, I met Isa on the second heaven. I found him of a medium stature, reddish white complexion. His body was so clean and clear that it appeared as though he had just performed Ghusl and come.*"

Sayyiduna Isa ﷺ will descend near the eastern minaret of the Umayyad mosque in Damascus, wearing two yellow sheets and leaning on the shoulders of two angels. His hair will be spread to the shoulders, straight, neat and shining. He will return as a follower of Sayyiduna Rasoolullah ﷺ and not a Prophet himself. He will join a group of righteous people, who will be preparing for war against Dajjal. It will be the time for Fajr prayer and Imaam Mahdi ﷺ will be the leader of the Muslims. Suddenly, a voice will be heard saying, "*One who listens to your pleas has come.*"

At the time of his arrival, Dajjal will already have emerged. Dajjal will start melting from the beautiful fragrance of Sayyiduna Isa's ﷺ breath, just like salt melting in water. Sayyiduna Isa ﷺ will chase him and kill him.

Sayyiduna Isa ﷺ will break the cross and kill the pigs during his time on earth. Allah ﷻ will end every other religion except for Islam. There will be peace and security on earth so that lions will be at peace with camels and children will be able to play with snakes without being harmed.

Sayyiduna Isa ﷺ will marry and have children. He will stay in this world for 40 years and will then pass away and will be laid to rest in the shrine next to our Prophet Muhammad ﷺ in the Prophet's ﷺ mosque in Al-Madinah Al-Munawwarah.

MAJOR SIGNS: YA'JOOJ AND MA'JOOJ

Ya'jooj and Ma'jooj (Gog and Magog) are an evil group of people who have been imprisoned behind a wall in an unknown valley.

Sayyiduna Dhul Qarnayn ﷺ was a pious person who Allah ﷻ had made a king. He was also a very just king who never oppressed anyone. As he conquered lands and spread the message of Allah ﷻ, he would invite people to the worship of one God. He once came across a people close to two towering mountains who were kind to each other.

The people told him *"Between these mountains, there is a nation called Ya'jooj and Ma'jooj, who are like animals. Their teeth are like those of wild animals. When they come out they eat snakes, scorpions, horses, mules, donkeys, vegetables and wild animals. We will give you something if you build a wall between Ya'jooj and Ma'jooj and us so that they won't harm us."*

The people offered to give Sayyiduna Dhul Qarnayn ﷺ a generous reward for his work but he refused saying "That which my Lord has given me is better." He also asked for a group of people to help him build the great wall. Sayyiduna Dhul Qarnayn ﷺ built a wall of iron so the tribes of Ya'jooj and Ma'jooj could neither climb over nor break through it.

Towards the end of time, Allah ﷻ will cause this wall to collapse and the tribe of Ya'jooj and Ma'jooj will escape. They will emerge once Sayyiduna Isa ﷺ kills Dajjal. Their number will be so large that when they pass by a lake the first of them will drink from it and by the time the last of them passes by the same lake there will be no water remaining and they will say, "Once there was water here."

They will kill and destroy everything that comes in their path. At the end of the killing and corruption, they will say, "We have killed all those on earth, now let us kill those in the sky." They will then fire their arrows towards the sky and through the will of Allah ﷻ, their arrows will return to the ground tipped with blood.

In the meantime, Sayyiduna Isa عليه السلام will be on Mount Tur (Sinai) with the Muslims. Sayyiduna Isa عليه السلام and the Muslims will make Duaa to Allah ﷻ to remove this difficulty and Allah ﷻ will create a worm in the necks of the Ya'jooj and Ma'jooj which will result in their death.

After the destruction of Ya'jooj and Ma'jooj, Sayyiduna Isa will descend with his followers from Mount Tur (Sinai).

They will not find a single piece of the earth which is not littered with the dead and rotting bodies of Ya'jooj and Ma'jooj.

Sayyiduna Isa عليه السلام and his followers will once again make Duaa to Allah ﷻ. He will send a huge bird which will pick up their remains and leave them wherever Allah ﷻ wills. The Muslims will set the spears, arrows and bows of Ya'jooj and Ma'jooj alight, which will burn continuously for 7 years. Allah ﷻ will then send a shower of rain which will cleanse and refresh the earth.

After the destruction of Ya'jooj and Ma'jooj, there will be a period of peace and prosperity.

Sayyiduna Dhul Qarnayn ﷺ teaches us the importance of being fair to people. If we are given money and wealth, then we should be grateful to Allah ﷻ. We can do this by speaking the truth and never swearing or lying. We also learn about the importance of helping people and inviting them to Islam.

The Prophet ﷺ said to Sayyiduna Ali ؓ, "If Allah guides a person through you, it is better for you than all that is in the world."

The Beast دَآبَّةُ الْأَرْضِ

> وَإِذَا وَقَعَ الْقَوْلُ عَلَيْهِمْ أَخْرَجْنَا لَهُمْ دَآبَّةً مِّنَ الْأَرْضِ تُكَلِّمُهُمْ أَنَّ النَّاسَ كَانُوا بِآيَاتِنَا لَا يُوقِنُونَ
>
> "And when the word befalls them, We will bring forth for them a creature from the earth speaking to them, [saying] that the people were, of Our verses, not certain [in faith]."
>
> Surah Al-Naml, Ayah No: 82

Amongst the very last signs of the final day, is the appearance of the Beast which will emerge from the earth. The Beast will be a creature who will look very unusual and will speak to the people as it travels throughout the world.

The beast will possess the staff of Sayyiduna Musa ؑ with which it will mark the faces of the believers causing their faces to shine. Whilst with the ring of Sayyiduna Sulaymaan ؑ, the beast will mark the faces of the disbelievers causing their faces to turn black. At this point, all the Muslims and disbelievers will clearly be identified and recognised. Once the creature finishes its duty, it will disappear.

EXERCISE FIVE

ANSWER THE QUESTIONS BELOW.

1. Write a short paragraph explaining what Sayyiduna Rasoolullah ﷺ said about Sayyiduna Isa عليه السلام, how long he will live for and where he will be put to rest.

_____
_____
_____
_____
_____
_____
_____

2. Explain, in your own words, how Gog and Magog came to be imprisoned behind the wall.

_____
_____
_____
_____
_____
_____

3. What did you learn from the character of Sayyiduna Dhul Qarnayn ﷺ?

_____
_____
_____
_____
_____
_____
_____

4. Explain the order in which the major signs will come about.

_____
_____
_____

5. If Sayyiduna Rasoolullah ﷺ is Khatam Al-Nabiyyeen and the last Prophet sent by Allah ﷻ then how do we explain the coming of Sayyiduna Isa عليه السلام after Sayyiduna Rasoolullah ﷺ.

_____
_____
_____
_____
_____
_____
_____
_____
_____
_____
_____
_____
_____
_____
_____
_____

LESSON SIX - DEATH

Everyone has to leave this world. Ultimately, death shall approach us and we shall no longer remain here, rather we will die and will present ourselves in the court of Allah ﷻ. Hence, we should prepare for our final destination where we shall live forever.

Our Prophet ﷺ says, "Live in this world as though you are a traveller, in fact like a passer-by."

A traveller is a stranger and does not engage himself in entertainment and fun. Likewise, a Muslim should not be entangled in this world and what is in it such that he forgets about his death. A person should also remember death in abundance, for our Prophet ﷺ remembered it regularly. We are reminded of death every day when we hear about people passing away. In the same way, people will one day hear about our passing away. When we hear about someone passing away we should say إِنَّا لِلَّهِ وَإِنَّا إِلَيْهِ رَاجِعُونَ.

Allah ﷻ says in the Qur'aan:

كُلُّ نَفْسٍ ذَائِقَةُ الْمَوْتِ وَإِنَّمَا تُوَفَّوْنَ أُجُورَكُمْ يَوْمَ الْقِيَامَةِ فَمَن زُحْزِحَ عَنِ النَّارِ وَأُدْخِلَ الْجَنَّةَ فَقَدْ فَازَ وَمَا الْحَيَاةُ الدُّنْيَا إِلَّا مَتَاعُ الْغُرُورِ

"Every soul will taste death, and you will only be given your [full] compensation on the Day of Resurrection. So he who is drawn away from the Fire and admitted to Paradise has attained [his desire]. And what is the life of this world except the enjoyment of delusion."

Surah Al-Imran, Ayah No: 185

Death is not the end for a person, rather it is just the beginning. When believers leave this world, they are placed in a grave. Two Angels named Munkar and Nakeer will descend into the person's grave. The person's soul will return into their body. Angels thereafter will ask the following questions:

1. Who is your lord?

2. What is your religion?

3. What did you say about this man (Sayyiduna Rasoolullah ﷺ) ?

A believer will reply, "My lord is Allah ﷻ, my religion is Islam and the person sent to me is the messenger of Allah ﷺ ".

A disbeliever will reply, "Alas, I don't know!" for all the questions that will be asked.

A believer who is able to answer Munkar and Nakeer's questions correctly will be given the bedding of Jannah. He will wear the clothes of Jannah and the gateway to Jannah will be shown to him. He will feel the cool and fragrant breeze of Jannah in his grave.

A disbeliever, who fails to answer Munkar and Nakeer's questions correctly, will be given a bedding of fire, clothing of fire and will be shown the gateway to the Hellfire. The dead person will feel burning heat and hot winds from this gateway.

People will stay in their graves until Allah ﷻ raises them on the Day of Judgement.

If we want to enjoy the sweet fragrance of Jannah in our grave then we need to start preparing for death. We can do this by always doing good actions and staying away from evil actions with our hands, feet, eyes and mouths.

EXERCISE SIX

ANSWER THE QUESTIONS BELOW.

1. Describe what happens when one answers the questions of Munkar and Nakeer correctly in the grave. Also, describe what happens if one is not able to answer the questions.

_____
_____
_____
_____
_____
_____

2. What does Allah ﷻ say about death in the Qur'aan and what does this mean?

_____
_____
_____
_____

3. Think about your own death. What actions will you complete in this life before going to the grave? How will you ensure that you can answer the questions in the grave?

_____
_____
_____

4. Create a bookmark or a postcard with the 3 questions asked in the grave and the answers of a believer. Use the space below to sketch your design.

LESSON SEVEN-DAY OF JUDGEMENT

Al-Qiyamah (The Day of Judgement) will come when all the signs become obvious. Allah ﷻ will command Sayyiduna Israfeel ﷺ to blow the horn twice. After blowing the horn for the first time, everything will be destroyed including Sayyiduna Israfeel ﷺ and the horn, only Allah ﷻ will remain. For He is the one who has always existed and will exist. Allah ﷻ cannot perish.

When Allah ﷻ wishes, He will bring Sayyiduna Israfeel ﷺ back to life and will recreate the horn. He will then order Sayyiduna Israfeel ﷺ to blow the horn again. As the horn is blown for the second time, everyone such as Humans, Angels and Jinn will be brought back to life.

Once everyone is brought back to life from their graves, they will gather in a big place carrying their book of deeds. The good and bad people will be separated from each other. On this day, the sun will be brought close so that it is only a mile above our heads. The ground will be made of copper and people will have to stand upon it with their bare feet. The heat of the sun will cause the people's brains to boil.

Everyone will be sweating in accordance with their sins. Some will be sweating up to their ankles, some up to their knees and others will be drowning in their own sweat. However, the pious servants of Allah ﷻ will not be sweating at all but will be under the shade of Allah ﷻ.

Everyone will have to answer five questions on the Day of Judgement. The questions will be:

1. How did you spend your life?
2. How did you spend your youth?
3. How did you earn your money?
4. How did you spend that money?
5. How did you act on your knowledge?

Everyone will have to answer for every single thing they did in this world. So before we do anything, we should think about how we will answer to Allah ﷻ on the Day of Judgement.

Al-Meezaan (The scale)
Everyone's actions, good and bad, will be weighed on a scale. Good deeds will be placed on one side of the scale and bad deeds on the other side of the scale. If one's good deeds are heavier than his bad deeds, then he will be admitted into Jannah. However, if one's bad deeds are heavier than his good deeds, then he will be thrown into the Hellfire.

People will seek help from others on the Day of Judgement. When they find that their bad deeds are heavier than their good deeds. They will seek out their friends, family and people they knew in the world but none will help them because everyone will only be worried about themselves.

Whilst all this is happening, the people who had an abundance of good deeds in this world will be happy and resting under Allah's ﷻ shade.

In order to get to Jannah, one will have to cross a bridge known as Al-Siraat. This bridge runs over the Hellfire. It is thinner than hair, sharper than a sword and it is so long that it could take thousands of years to cross.

People will pass over the bridge in accordance with their deeds in the world. Some will pass over it with the speed of a flash of lightning. Some will pass over it like wind travelling at high speed. Some will pass over it as fast as birds, whilst others will pass over it with the speed of a fast horse. Yet others will pass over as slow as ants. Many people will plunge into the fire of Hell. The Day of Judgement will take fifty thousand years to pass and it will be a day of great torment and difficulty.

On that day, the only hope for people will be the intercession of Sayyiduna Rasoolullah ﷺ. When the people find themselves in such difficulty, they will seek help from Sayyiduna Adam ﷺ and Sayyiduna Nuh ﷺ. Eventually, they will turn to Rasoolullah ﷺ who will ask Allah ﷻ for permission to intercede so that He can save the people of his Ummah from being thrown into the Hellfire.

EXERCISE SEVEN

ANSWER THE QUESTIONS BELOW.

1. Who will blow the horn?
_____

2. What are the five questions that we will all be asked on the Day of Judgement?
_____
_____
_____
_____
_____

3. How will someone going to hell answer the question, "How did you spend your life?"
_____
_____
_____
_____
_____

4. Write down three things you can do to ensure that you will find the Day of Judgement easy?
_____
_____

5. If someone has done bad deeds in this world, how can they ensure that they will find the Day of Judgement easy? If they have done bad things to other people, then what should they do to make up for the bad things they did? Use examples in your answer.

حَدَّثَنَا النَّضْرُ بْنُ أَنَسِ بْنِ مَالِكٍ، عَنْ أَبِيهِ، قَالَ سَأَلْتُ النَّبِيَّ صلى الله عليه وسلم أَنْ يَشْفَعَ لِي يَوْمَ الْقِيَامَةِ فَقَالَ "أَنَا فَاعِلٌ". قَالَ قُلْتُ يَا رَسُولَ اللَّهِ فَأَيْنَ أَطْلُبُكَ قَالَ "اطْلُبْنِي أَوَّلَ مَا تَطْلُبُنِي عَلَى الصِّرَاطِ". قَالَ قُلْتُ فَإِنْ لَمْ أَلْقَكَ عَلَى الصِّرَاطِ قَالَ "فَاطْلُبْنِي عِنْدَ الْمِيزَانِ". قُلْتُ فَإِنْ لَمْ أَلْقَكَ عِنْدَ الْمِيزَانِ قَالَ "فَاطْلُبْنِي عِنْدَ الْحَوْضِ فَإِنِّي لاَ أُخْطِئُ هَذِهِ الثَّلاَثَ الْمَوَاطِنَ"

An-Nadr bin Anas bin Malik ﷺ narrated from his father who said:

"I asked the Prophet to intercede for me on the Day of Judgement. He said: 'I am the one to do so.'" [He said:] "I said: 'O Messenger of Allah! Then where shall I seek you?' He said: 'Seek me, the first time you should seek me is on the Siraat.'" [He said:] "I said: 'If I do not meet you upon the Siraat?' He said: 'Then seek me at the Meezan.' I said: 'And if I do not meet you at the Meezan?' He said: 'Then seek me at the Hawd, for indeed I will not be absent at these three places.'"

Al-Tirmidhi

LESSON EIGHT-JANNAH (PARADISE)

Jannah is a beautiful and vast place which Allah ﷻ has created for the believers. It is a place of such beauty that no eye has ever seen, no ear has ever heard and no mind has ever imagined anything like it.

The Ummah of our beloved Prophet Muhammad ﷺ will enter Jannah first, followed by everyone else and they will all be welcomed by Angels. The walls of Jannah have been made with bricks of gold and silver and its cement is made of musk. The ground is made of saffron. Instead of gravel, there will be diamonds and pearls. There are huge mansions made of pearls and diamonds to house the residents of Jannah.

There are four rivers in Jannah flowing with water, milk, wine and honey. All the residents will have these rivers running beneath their palaces. The wine of Jannah is not like the wine we find in the world, rather, it is pure from intoxicants and bad odour.

The trees of Jannah will have the most delicious fruit. There will be lush trees that will bear fruits which are not seen in this world. The fruits on these trees will hang so low that a person may pick them while standing, sitting or even when lying down. The most beautiful animals and birds of Jannah will live peacefully side by side.

The greatest blessing of Jannah will be seeing Allah ﷻ every morning and evening. When the believers enter Jannah, Allah ﷻ will ask if they desire anything else to which the believers will reply, *"You have brightened our faces and allowed us to enter Jannah. You freed us from Jahannam, now there is nothing else we desire."* Then the veils will be lifted and the believers will witness the countenance of Allah ﷻ.

There shall be no impurities in Jannah, meaning there will be no urine, stool or mucus. The clothing of the people of Jannah will never become old or worn out and the residents will remain young forever. The people of Jannah will forever live in harmony without disagreement, hatred or jealousy amongst them. Those in Paradise will not find the need to sleep as it is a form of death.

The people of paradise will have the opportunity to partake in all the delicacies provided in Jannah. Whatever they desire will appear before them without any effort. If a resident of Jannah sees a bird and wishes to taste its meat, it will appear cooked before them immediately.

ACTIONS THAT WILL TAKE US INTO JANNAH

1. Believing in Allah ﷻ and performing good deeds:

Allah ﷻ says:

"Give glad tidings to those who believe and do good deeds that for them are gardens beneath which rivers flow."

(Surah Baqarah 2:25)

If we believe in Allah ﷻ and try our utmost to follow His commands then Allah ﷻ promises us a place in Jannah.

2. To obey our Prophet's ﷺ Sunnah:

Our Prophet ﷺ says "The one who loves my Sunnah has loved me and the one who loves me will be with me in Jannah."

One cannot truly obey Allah without adhering to the Sunnah of our Beloved Prophet ﷺ in all matters.

Here are some actions mentioned by Our Prophet ﷺ that we should strive to perform:

3. Visiting the sick:

'Whoever visits a sick person, a caller calls from heaven: 'May you be happy, may your walking be blessed, and may you occupy a dignified position in Paradise.'"

4. Spreading Salaam:

Abdullah Ibn Salam ؓ narrates that the very first words the Messenger ﷺ spoke when he arrived in Al-Madinah Al-Munawwarah were, "O people, spread peace, share food, pray during the night while others sleep and you will enter Jannah in peace." (Al-Tirmidhi)

5. Sunnah Prayers:

Whoever offers 12 Rakahs in the day and night, Allah ﷻ will build for him a house in Jannah:

- 2 Rakahs before Fajr
- 4 Rakahs before Dhuhr
- 2 Rakahs after Dhuhr
- 2 Rakahs after Maghrib
- 2 Rakahs after Isha

(Sahih Muslim)

6. In Surah Al-Mu'minoon, Allah ﷻ tells us that the people who will be residents of Jannah will be those that:

- Are humble when offering Salah
- Stay away from vain things which waste time.
- Give Zakah.
- Keep their promises.
- Are punctual with their Salah.

EXERCISE EIGHT

ANSWER THE QUESTIONS BELOW.

1. Write 8 words that come to mind when you think of Jannah.

2. Which 4 rivers will be found in Jannah?

   _____   _____

   _____   _____

3. How will the believers be welcomed into Jannah?

   _____
   _____
   _____
   _____

4. Describe the palaces found in Jannah.

_____
_____
_____
_____

5. Jannah is one of the best rewards for obeying and worshipping Allah ﷻ in this world. Imagine yourself in Jannah and you are remembering your life in this world. Write down a list of 4 things you always did in this world and 4 things you always stayed away from, which helped you enter Jannah.

Things you always did
1._____
2._____
3._____
4._____

Things you stayed away from
1._____
2._____
3._____
4._____

LESSON NINE-JAHANNAM (HELL)

Jahannam is a place of pain and grief, which has been prepared by Allah ﷻ for the disbelievers, hypocrites and the sinful. The lightest punishment in Jahannam will boil the brains of its inhabitants. There will also be snakes and scorpions biting the inhabitants of hell.

Jahannam was heated for a thousand years and its fire turned red. It was then heated for another thousand years before the fire turned white. It was again heated for another thousand years and it turned black. At present, Jahannam is pitch black and totally dark.

Once people are thrown into Jahannam, they will face some scary and terrifying angels. These angels never smile and they will have no mercy on the wrong doers. The angels will ask the sinners what excuse they have for being here. No one will dare speak a lie in front of these angels, instead they will admit that they have no excuses. The gates will then be closed and locked.

The punishment of Jahannam is very scary and we must always remember that these punishments are not just for the disbelievers but also for those Muslims who are sinful and do not follow the religion. The only thing that will save them is if Allah ﷻ decides to forgive them. Therefore, we should always seek to repent to Allah ﷻ from any sins and intend to never commit those sins again to save ourselves from Jahannam.

The inhabitants of hell will be fed boiling water which will be poured on their heads. It will pierce their skulls until it reaches their stomachs. This will make their guts melt and go down to their feet. After this, their bodies will be returned to its original form so the punishment can be repeated.

EXERCISE NINE

ANSWER THE QUESTIONS BELOW.

1. List the three types of people who will be punished in Jahannam.

_____
_____
_____

2. Describe the lightest punishment in Jahannam.

_____
_____
_____

3. Describe the things about Jahannam that you dislike the most.

_____
_____
_____
_____
_____

4. What actions will you take to ensure that you are save from Jahannam?

_____
_____
_____
_____
_____

5. Compare Jannah and Jahannam in your own words. Imagine you entered Jannah. Describe the things you will have done in this world to ensure that Allah ﷻ grants you Jannah.

_____
_____
_____
_____
_____
_____
_____
_____
_____
_____
_____
_____
_____

Qamar Learning Academy

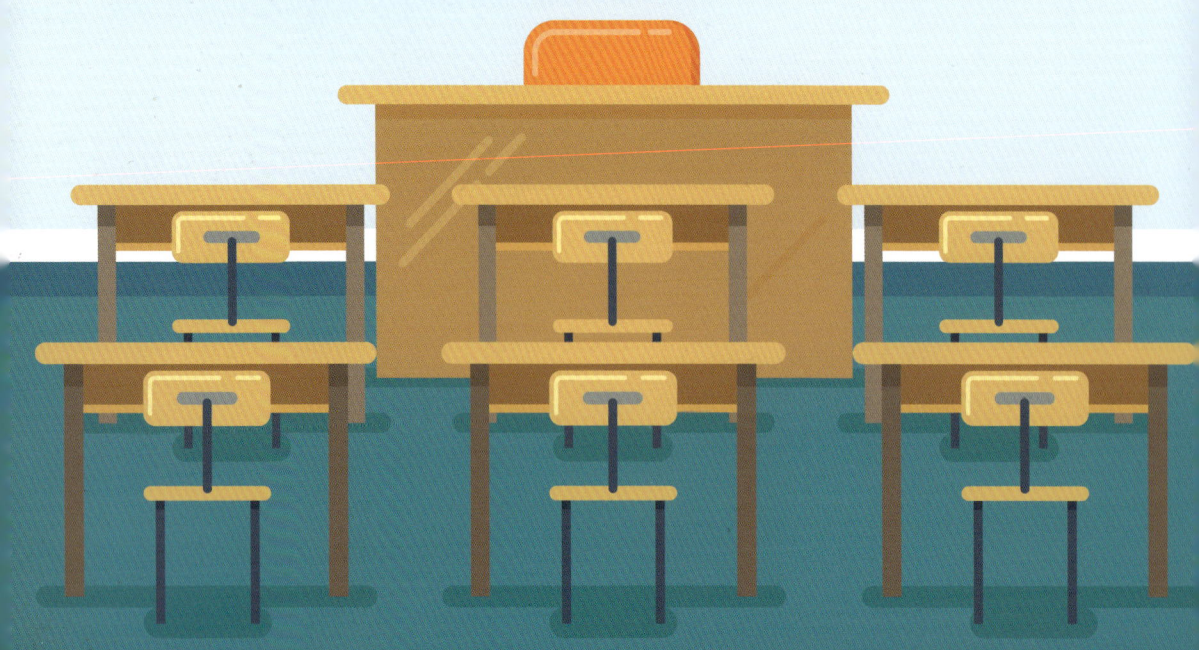

اَلْفِقُه

What's in this section?

FIQH (HANAFI)

TYPES OF IMPURITY
- Rules of Impurity

GHUSL
- Fardh acts of Ghusl
- Sunnah method of Ghusl
- Makrooh acts of Ghusl

WUDHU
- Method of Wudhu
- Faraidh of Wudhu
- Sunnah acts of Wudhu
- Makrooh acts of Wudhu
- Acts that nullify Wudhu

TAYAMMUM
- How to perform Tayammum
- Fardh acts of Tayammum
- Sunnah acts of Tayammum

TIMES OF SALAH
- Disliked prayer times
- The daily prayers

SALAH
- The conditions of Salah
- Fardh acts of Salah
- Model prayer
- Wajib acts of Salah
- Sunnah acts of Salah

BREAKERS AND MAKROOH ACTS OF SALAH

SAJDAH AL-SAHW

PRAYER OF A MASBOOQ

THE DAY OF JUMU'AH

FASTING

HAJJ (THE PILGRIMAGE)

LESSON ONE - TYPES OF IMPURITY (NAJASAH)

A Muslim always stays clean and pure.

> Our Prophet Muhammad ﷺ has taught us that:
>
> اَلطُّهُورُ شَطْرُ الْإِيمَانِ
>
> (Al-Muslim) *"Cleanliness is half of faith"*

Some acts of worship, such as Salah, are not accepted by Allah ﷻ unless they are performed whilst one is clean. Najasah is the term used for impurity; mentioned within the Qur'aan or Hadith.

There are two types of impurity:

1. Najasah Ghaleezah: Major impurity

The following types of impurity are Najasah Ghaleezah.

Najasah Ghaleezah in humans

- Urine
- Flowing blood
- Water flowing from an infected eye
- Vomit which is more than a mouthful
- Stool
- Pus

Najasah Ghaleezah in animals that are Halal to eat

- Stool
  - ➢ Exception: The droppings of all birds is not impure apart from fowls and ducks whose droppings are Najasah Ghaleezah.
- Flowing blood from a land animal
- Flesh and fat of animals that were not slaughtered in the Halal way

Najasah Ghaleezah in animals that are Haraam to eat

- Urine
- Blood
- Stool
- Saliva
- Flesh and fat
- All parts of a pig

> Exception: Cat saliva is not impure but cats are still Haraam to eat.

Other types of Najasah Ghaleezah

- All alcoholic drinks e.g. wine/beer etc.

2. Najasah Khafeefah: Minor impurity

The following types of impurity are Najasah Khafeefah.

Types of Najasah Khafeefah

- Urine of all animals that are Halaal to eat, e.g. cow, goat, horse etc.
- Droppings of birds that are Haraam to eat, e.g. crow, kite, falcon etc.

RULES OF IMPURITY

The person intending to pray must remove impurity from their body, garments and place of prayer. The boxes below help us to understand how to deal with different types of impurity.

Najasah Ghaleezah

| If the impurity is greater than the size of a dirham (i.e. Size of a 2p coin) | → | The impurity is more than the excusable amount and it is Fardh to clean it. Prayer is not valid and must be repeated. |

| If the impurity is equal to the size of a dirham (i.e. Size of a 2p coin) | → | It is Wajib to clean it. If Salah is performed without cleaning the impurity then it is Makrooh and it is Wajib to repeat the prayer. |

| If the impurity is less than the size of a dirham (i.e. Size of a 2p coin) | → | It is excused; however, it is Sunnah to remove the impurity. If one performs Salah without cleaning the impurity then the prayer will still be valid. |

Najasah Khafeefah

| If the impurity is less than a quarter of the part of the garment (eg. sleeve) or the body (eg. hand) on which it falls. | → | It is excused. However, it is Sunnah to remove the impurity. If one performs Salah without cleaning the impurity then the prayer will still be valid. |

| If the impurity is more than a quarter of the part of the garment (eg. sleeve) or the body (eg. hand) on which it falls. | → | The impurity is more than the excusable amount, it is Fardh to clean it. Prayer is not valid and must be repeated. |

Method of cleansing the body and garments from impurities

The following are different methods of cleansing:

- Impurity can be removed with water or any other cleansing liquid eg. Vinegar. If the impurity is visible, all traces of it must be removed. However, if the impurity is not visible, the area must be washed thoroughly three times.
- Any surface where the impurity cannot penetrate such as glass, should be cleaned by wiping the surface.
- If the ground has any impurity on it and it has dried out leaving no visible trace, the ground is pure and it is permissible to pray on.

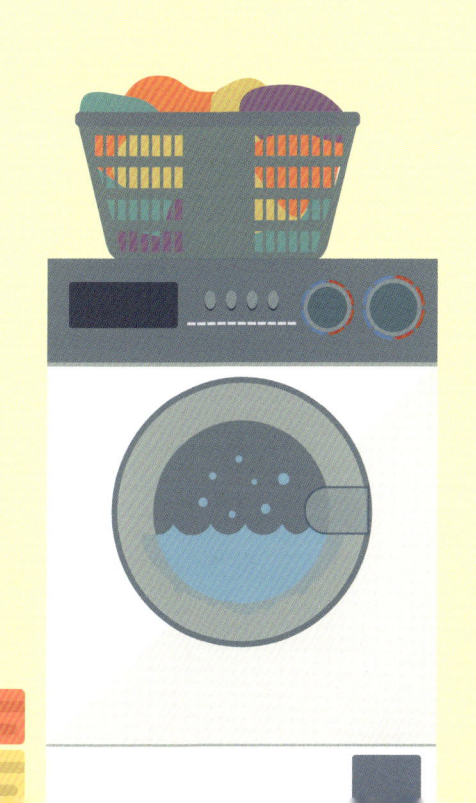

EXERCISE ONE

CIRCLE THE CORRECT TYPE OF IMPURITY FOR EACH OF THE ITEMS BELOW.

Urine of a cow
Ghaleezah | Neither | Khafeefah

Human saliva
Ghaleezah | Neither | Khafeefah

Stool of a goat
Ghaleezah | Neither | Khafeefah

Stool of a pigeon
Ghaleezah | Neither | Khafeefah

Stool of an eagle
Ghaleezah | Neither | Khafeefah

A mouthful of vomit of a baby
Ghaleezah | Neither | Khafeefah

Coca Cola
Ghaleezah | Neither | Khafeefah

Saliva of a pig
Ghaleezah | Neither | Khafeefah

Flowing blood of a cat
Ghaleezah | Neither | Khafeefah

Flesh of a non-halal chicken
Ghaleezah | Neither | Khafeefah

Urine of a horse
Ghaleezah | Neither | Khafeefah

Tomato Ketchup
Ghaleezah | Neither | Khafeefah

Rainwater
Ghaleezah | Neither | Khafeefah

Wine
Ghaleezah | Neither | Khafeefah

عَنْ أَبِي مَالِكٍ الْأَشْعَرِيِّ قَالَ قَالَ رَسُولُ اللهِ صَلَّى اللهُ عَلَيْهِ وَسَلَّمَ الطُّهُورُ شَطْرُ الْإِيمَانِ. وَالْحَمْدُ لِلَّهِ تَمْلَأُ الْمِيزَانَ. وَسُبْحَانَ اللهِ وَالْحَمْدُ لِلَّهِ تَمْلَآَنِ. أَوْ تَمْلَأُ مَا بَيْنَ السَّمَاوَاتِ وَالْأَرْضِ وَالصَّلَاةُ نُورٌ. وَالصَّدَقَةُ بُرْهَانٌ. وَالصَّبْرُ ضِيَاءٌ. وَالْقُرْآنُ حُجَّةٌ لَكَ أَوْ عَلَيْكَ كُلُّ النَّاسِ يَغْدُو فَبَايِعٌ نَفْسَهُ فَمُعْتِقُهَا أَوْ مُوبِقُهَا

"Purity is half of faith, and the praise of Allah fills the scale. Glorification and praise fill up what is between the heavens and the earth. Prayer is a light, charity is proof, and patience is illumination. The Qur'aan is a proof for you or against you. All people go out early in the morning and sell themselves, either setting themselves free or destroying themselves."

Sahih Muslim

LESSON TWO - GHUSL

Ghusl means to wash the entire body in order to become pure. Allah says in the Qur'aan

> وَإِنْ كُنْتُمْ جُنُبًا فَاطَّهَّرُوا
>
> *"If you are impure, then purify yourselves"*
>
> Surah: Al-Maidah, Ayah no: 6

The Fardh acts of Ghusl

1. Rinse the whole mouth;

2. Rinse and clean the inside of the nose up to the top of the nostrils;

3. Wash the entire body once so that no part of the body remains dry.

NOTE: If any of the above Fardh acts of Ghusl are missed, Ghusl will not be valid.

The Sunnah method of Ghusl

1. Make intention.

> نَوَيْتُ اَنْ اَغْتَسِلَ لِرَفْعِ الْحَدَثِ
>
> I make intention to perform Ghusl for the removal of impurity.

2. Wash both hands including the wrists.
3. Wash the private parts.
4. Remove all dirt or impurities from the body.
5. Perform Wudhu ensuring the mouth and nose are rinsed.
6. Pour water over the entire body three times beginning with the head, followed by the right shoulder, the left shoulder and the remainder of the whole body starting with the right limb each time.
7. As water is poured, rub the body to ensure no part is left dry.

Makrooh Acts of Ghusl

- Wasting water.
- Using more water than required.
- Talking unnecessarily.
- To start washing with the left limb as opposed to the right.
- Extending the feet towards the Qiblah.
- Cleaning the nose using the right hand.

Important points for Ghusl

- Girls who have plaits are not required to undo them but it is important to make sure water reaches the roots of their hair.
- If there are any substances such as nail varnish, super glue or jewellery preventing water reaching the skin, it must be removed before performing Ghusl.

EXERCISE TWO

ANSWER THE QUESTIONS BELOW.

1. List the three Faraidh of Ghusl.

   _____
   _____
   _____

2. Saami is performing Ghusl and starts by washing his entire body, such that no part of his skin remains dry.

   He finishes his Ghusl without doing anything else.

   Is Saami's Ghusl valid? Explain your answer.

   _____
   _____
   _____
   _____
   _____

3. Faatima performs Ghusl without removing her rings which are so tight that they do not allow water to pass under them.

   Is Faatima's Ghusl valid? Explain your answer

   _____
   _____
   _____
   _____

4. Ibrahim is performing Ghusl. As he is performing Wudhu, he feels the need to relieve himself and goes to the toilet to urinate. He then continues his Wudhu from where he left off and completes his Ghusl. Is Ibrahim's Ghusl valid? Explain your answer.

_____
_____
_____
_____
_____
_____

5. A man falls into a flowing river and all of his body is drenched by the water to the extent that his mouth and nostrils are all fully wet. Is his Ghusl valid? Explain your answer.

_____
_____
_____
_____
_____
_____

LESSON THREE-WUDHU

Method of Wudhu

Wudhu is an important part of a Muslim's ritual of purity. Our Prophet Muhammad ﷺ taught us that it is the key to Salah.

> **Make Niyyah of Wudhu:**
>
> اَتَوَضَّأُ لِرَفْعِ الْحَدَثِ أَعُوْذُ بِاللهِ مِنَ الشَّيْطَانِ الرَّجِيْمِ بِسْمِ اللهِ الرَّحْمٰنِ الرَّحِيْمِ بِسْمِ اللهِ وَالْحَمْدُ لِلّٰهِ عَلٰى دِيْنِ الْإِسْلَامِ
>
> I perform Wudhu to remove minor impurity. I seek refuge in Allah ﷻ from the rejected Shaytaan. In the name of Allah ﷻ, the beneficent the most merciful. In the name of Allah ﷻ, all praise is for Allah ﷻ for the faith of Islam.

1. Wash your hands, including the wrists, three times; first the right then the left.

2. Use a Miswak (tooth stick), toothbrush or finger. Wash your mouth and gargle three times.

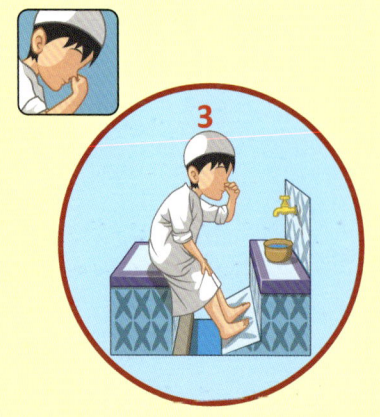

3. Rinse your nose three times using the right hand and clean it using the left.

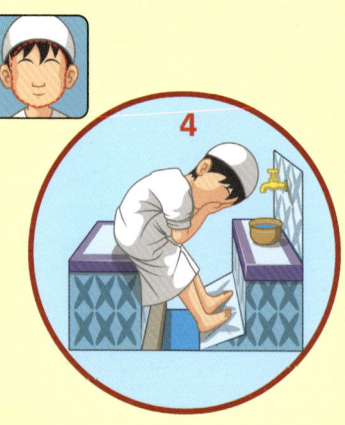

4. Wash the entire face three times from the top of the forehead to the bottom of the chin and from one earlobe to the other.

5

Wash your arms up to and including the elbows three times; first your right arm then your left.

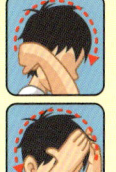

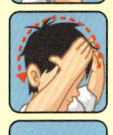

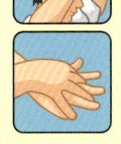

6

Wet both hands once and using the middle, ring and small fingers, wipe the head starting from the front and ending at the back. Next, using your palms, wipe the sides of the head returning from the back to the front.

Clean the inner parts of your ears using your index fingers and clean the back of your ears with your thumbs.

Wipe your nape (back of the neck) once using the back part of your hands. Perform Khilaal of both the hands meaning to pass wet fingers between each other.

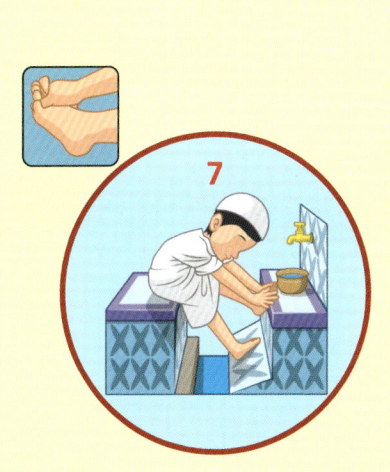

7

Wash your feet up to and including the ankles three times; first your right then your left. Perform Khilaal of your toes by passing wet fingers between them.

اَشْهَدُ اَنْ لَّا إِلَهَ إِلَّا اللهُ وَحْدَهُ لَا شَرِيكَ لَهُ،
وَاَشْهَدُ اَنَّ مُحَمَّداً عَبْدُهُ وَرَسُولُهُ
اَللَّهُمَّ اجْعَلْنِي مِنَ التَّوَّابِينَ
وَاجْعَلْنِي مِنَ الْمُتَطَهِّرِينَ

8

Finally, recite the following Duaa which is Masnoon, which means that it comes from our Prophet Muhammad ﷺ "I testify that there is no God but Allah. He is alone, has no partner and I testify that Muhammad is his servant and Messenger."

"O Allah, make me from those who repent and those who purify themselves."

P a g e | 81

FARAIDH OF WUDHU

In Wudhu, there are some actions that are obligatory (Fardh), others that the Prophet ﷺ performed, approved or liked (Sunnah) and those that are disliked (Makrooh).

> يَـٰٓأَيُّهَا ٱلَّذِينَ ءَامَنُوٓا۟ إِذَا قُمْتُمْ إِلَى ٱلصَّلَوٰةِ فَٱغْسِلُوا۟ وُجُوهَكُمْ وَأَيْدِيَكُمْ إِلَى ٱلْمَرَافِقِ وَٱمْسَحُوا۟ بِرُءُوسِكُمْ وَأَرْجُلَكُمْ إِلَى ٱلْكَعْبَيْنِ
>
> "Believers, when you are about to pray, wash your face, your hands and arms including the elbows, wipe your head and wash your feet including the ankles."
>
> Surah: Al-Maidah, Ayah no: 6

Faraidh of Wudhu

- To wash the entire face once from the top of the forehead to the bottom of the chin and from one earlobe to the other earlobe.

- To wash both arms up to and including the elbows once starting with your right arm and then the left arm.

- To perform Masah (wiping of the head) once. This means to wet both hands and wipe at least a quarter of your head with them.

- To wash both feet, including the ankles, once and between the toes.

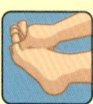

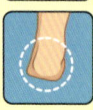

SUNNAH ACTS OF WUDHU

We must act upon the Sunnah actions of Wudhu as they bring us reward.

What are the Sunnah acts of Wudhu?

- To make intention for Wudhu.
- To recite Tasmiyah. بِسْمِ اللّٰهِ الرَّحْمٰنِ الرَّحِيْمِ
- To wash both hands, including the wrists, three times.
- To clean the teeth using a Miswak.
- To wash the mouth and gargle three times using the right hand.
- To sniff water into the nose using the right hand and cleaning the inside of the nose with the left hand three times.
- To make Khilaal of the beard, meaning to pass wet fingers through the beard.
- To make Khilaal of the fingers and toes.
- To wash each limb three times.
- To make Masah of the whole head once.
- To make Masah of both ears once.
- To wash each limb in the correct order.
- To begin washing each limb with the right side first.
- To wash each limb one after the other without delaying to ensure the previous limb does not dry up before washing the next one.
- To recite the Sunnah Duaa after the completion of Wudhu. اَللّٰهُمَّ اجْعَلْنِيْ مِنَ التَّوَّابِيْنَ وَ اجْعَلْنِيْ مِنَ الْمُتَطَهِّرِيْنَ

MAKROOH ACTS OF WUDHU

THERE ARE CERTAIN ACTS WHICH ARE DISLIKED (MAKROOH) WHEN PERFORMING WUDHU. THESE ACTS DECREASE THE REWARD OF WUDHU AND WE SHOULD AVOID THEM. HOWEVER, THE WUDHU WILL STILL BE VALID AND DOES NOT NEED TO BE REPEATED.

What are the Makrooh acts in Wudhu?

- To waste water and to use more than is needed.

- To use too little water so that water does not flow over the skin.

- To wash the face by splashing water on it with force or washing the face using only one hand.

- To talk unnecessarily when performing Wudhu.

- To wash the left side before the right side of any limb.

- To extend the feet towards the Qiblah when washing them.

- To rinse the nose using the right hand.

ACTS THAT NULLIFY WUDHU

If you want to pray Salah, touch the Qur'aan or perform Tawaaf of the Ka'bah you must be in the state of Wudhu. There are certain actions which break Wudhu:

To pass urine, stool or wind.

The flow of blood or pus from the body.

To vomit a mouthful (If a person vomits blood or pus, it nullifies Wudhu even if it is less than a mouthful).

To sleep lying on the side, resting on the hand or leaning. However, sleeping whilst standing, bowing, prostrating or sitting does not nullify Wudhu.

To become unconscious or insane.

To laugh out loud whilst performing Salah.

Blood appearing in the mouth. However Wudhu only breaks if there is more blood than saliva.

EXERCISE THREE

ANSWER THE QUESTIONS BELOW.

Zaid and Adam went to the mosque to pray Maghrib. After the prayer, they both sat at the back of the mosque leaning against the wall listening to the imam deliver a lecture. Zaid fell asleep only to be woken by Adam nudging him because he was snoring loudly. The time was close to Isha and Zaid gets up to pray. Adam tells him he needs to perform Wudhu. They begin to argue at the back of the mosque. What should Zaid do?

_____

_____

_____

_____

Zaid and Adam are performing ablution together. After Wudhu and after they have prayed Salah, Zaid is unsure whether he washed his mouth and gargled. He discusses this with Adam who is convinced he needs to repeat his Wudhu and that they both must repeat their prayer because Zaid had led the prayer. Adam then adds that he remembers that he had only washed his face once. What should they both do?

_____

_____

_____

_____

Samuel enters the Wudhu area and finds Abu Bakr and Ibrahim performing Wudhu. Ibrahim turns to Abu Bakr and starts talking about the football match they had watched earlier in the day. Abu Bakr remains silent and continues to perform Wudhu. Abu Bakr then throws water on Ibrahim before completing his Wudhu. Samuel then performed Wudhu but his right elbow was still dry when he finished.

3a) Did all three boys perform Wudhu correctly? Please explain your answer.

_____
_____
_____
_____
_____
_____

The three of them then enter the mosque to perform Salah. Abu Bakr leads them in prayer.

3b) In the boxes below, place a tick next to the name of the person whose prayer is valid and a cross next to the name of the person whose prayer is not valid.

Name	✓ ✗
Abu Bakr	
Samuel	
Ibrahim	

LESSON FOUR - TAYAMMUM

Tayammum means Dry Ablution and is another way of purifying ourselves like performing Wudhu or Ghusl.

Tayammum is performed instead of Wudhu or Ghusl when:

There is no water to be found within a mile radius.	A person is very sick and fears that the use of water will cause more illness or harm.	A person only has enough water for drinking but not enough for Wudhu.
A person is late for a funeral prayer or Eid prayer and fears that they will miss the prayer if they perform Wudhu.	A person fears that they will be attacked by a snake or any other animal if they try to fetch water for Wudhu.	The water is very cold and there is no way to heat it whilst it is considered highly probable that using the water may cause harm.

How to perform Tayammum

1. Begin by making the intention to perform Tayammum.
2. Strike both hands on a surface like sand or soil.
3. Pass both hands over the face once making sure the area between the forehead and the chin and the area between both earlobes has been covered by the hands.
4. Strike both hands on a surface like sand or soil.
5. Wipe both arms including the elbows once. Wipe the right arm with the left hand first followed by wiping the left arm with the right hand.

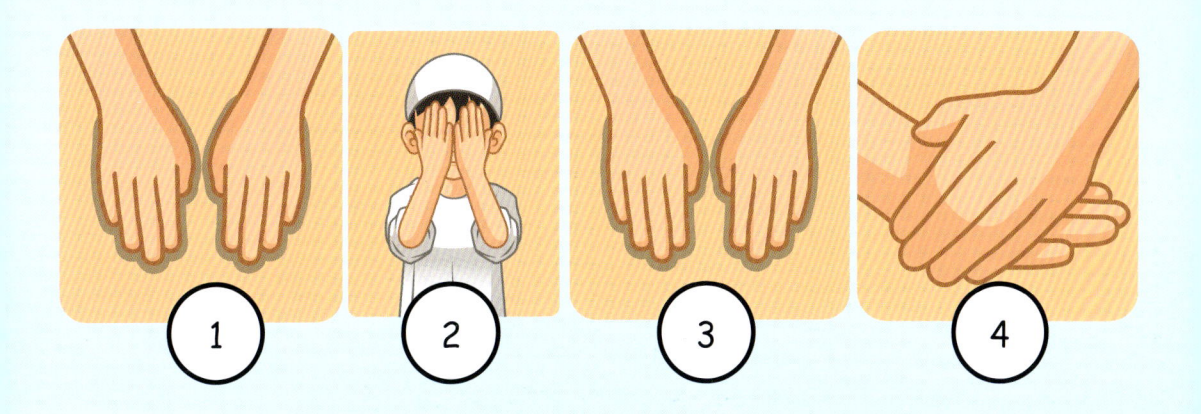

Fardh acts of Tayammum

There are 3 Fardh acts of Tayammum:

- Making the intention before performing Tayammum.
- Striking both hands and performing Masah of the face.
- Striking both hands and performing Masah of the arms including the elbows.

Sunnah acts when performing Tayammum

- Begin by reciting Tasmiyah.
- Maintain the sequence as mentioned in the Qur'aan.
- Continuity; so there is no delay between each step.
- Strike the surface firmly with the palms of the hands and shake or blow off any dust or earth.
- Spread the fingers when striking the ground.
- Rub the hands on the surface by first moving them forwards then backwards.

Surfaces on which Tayammum is permitted

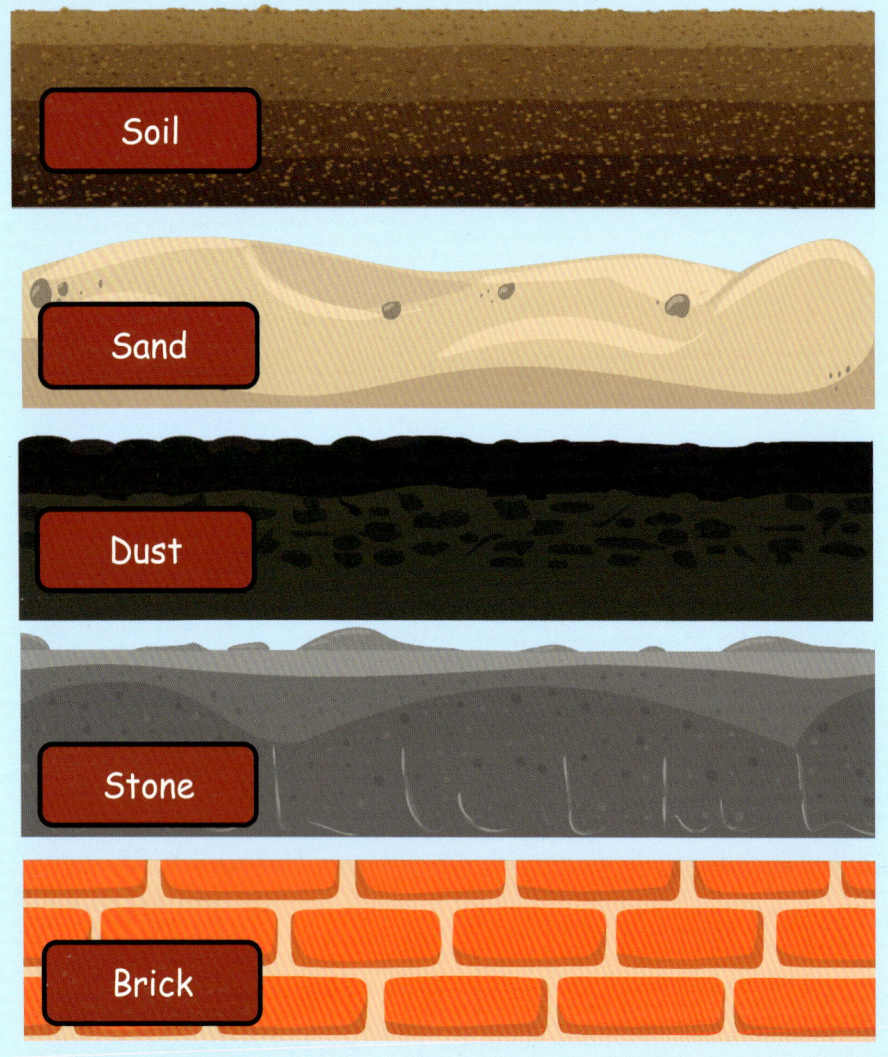

- Soil
- Sand
- Dust
- Stone
- Brick

Note: Tayammum is not permitted on: wood, glass, metal, food or any items which burn to ash, rot or melt, such as plastic.

- All actions which break Wudhu will break Tayammum.
- If one performs Tayammum due to an illness, it will break as soon as the illness is cured.
- Tayammum breaks on finding or regaining the ability to use water.

EXERCISE FOUR

ANSWER THE QUESTIONS BELOW.

1. The water board sends out leaflets saying that the water supply will be turned off from 10am until 5pm for the whole of the town.

When Dhuhr time begins, Aaishah performs Tayammum at the beginning of Dhuhr time but Aaminah delays performing the Dhuhr prayer for some time hoping the water will come back on before the time for Dhuhr ends. Asr time begins at 4pm.

Who is right? Explain your answer

_____
_____
_____
_____

2. Shahid left work late for Jumu'ah Salah. As he reaches the mosque he breaks his Wudhu. He does not have enough time to perform Wudhu but he finds some soil and performs Tayammum to catch the prayer.

Is his prayer valid or not? Explain your answer.

_____
_____
_____
_____

3. Sarah is climbing a mountain with her friend Aabidah. Sarah sits leaning with the palms of her hands on a rock. Once she removes her hands, she realises that there is no water and she must perform Tayammum in order to complete her Dhuhr Salah. As she has just rubbed her palms on a rock, she rubs them over her face and arms and tells Aabidah that her Tayammum is complete.

Aabidah is not sure. Advise Aabidah and Sarah about the validity of Sarah's Tayammum and write down what they both must do in order to complete their Dhuhr Salah. Explain your answer.

_____
_____
_____
_____
_____
_____
_____
_____
_____
_____
_____
_____
_____

أُعْطِيتُ خَمْسًا لَمْ يُعْطَهُنَّ أَحَدٌ قَبْلِي نُصِرْتُ بِالرُّعْبِ مَسِيرَةَ شَهْرٍ، وَجُعِلَتْ لِيَ الأَرْضُ مَسْجِدًا وَطَهُورًا، فَأَيُّمَا رَجُلٍ مِنْ أُمَّتِي أَدْرَكَتْهُ الصَّلاَةُ فَلْيُصَلِّ، وَأُحِلَّتْ لِيَ الْمَغَانِمُ وَلَمْ تَحِلَّ لِأَحَدٍ قَبْلِي، وَأُعْطِيتُ الشَّفَاعَةَ، وَكَانَ النَّبِيُّ يُبْعَثُ إِلَى قَوْمِهِ خَاصَّةً، وَبُعِثْتُ إِلَى النَّاسِ عَامَّةً

The Prophet said, "I have been given five things which were not given to anyone else before me.
1. Allah made me victorious by awe, (by His frightening my enemies) for a distance of one month's journey.
2. The earth has been made for me (and for my followers) a place for praying and a thing to perform Tayammum, therefore anyone of my followers can pray wherever the time of a prayer is due.
3. The booty has been made Halal (lawful) for me yet it was not lawful for anyone else before me.
4. I have been given the right of intercession (on the Day of Resurrection).
5. Every Prophet used to be sent to his nation only but I have been sent to all mankind.

Sahih Al-Bukhari

LESSON FIVE - TIMES OF SALAH

Each prayer has a specific time in which it must be performed.

Fajr (Dawn prayer): Fajr begins at the start of the true dawn (Subh Sadiq). True dawn is when light first appears in the sky. This light is visible in the east. Fajr ends when the sun begins to rise above the horizon.

Dhuhr (Noon prayer): Dhuhr begins after Zawaal (when the sun is at its highest point in the sky). It ends when the shadow of an object becomes twice its original length. This length is known as Mithlayn.

Asr (Mid-afternoon prayer): Asr begins at the end of Dhuhr time and ends as soon as the sun disappears below the horizon.

Maghrib (Sunset prayer): Maghrib begins when the sun disappears below the horizon and ends when dusk appears. Dusk is the moment just before total darkness in the sky.

Isha (Nightfall prayer): Isha begins at the end of Maghrib when there is total darkness in the sky and ends at the beginning of Fajr.

DISLIKED PRAYER TIMES

The Prophet ﷺ said, *"Do not perform Salah at the time the sun is rising or as it is setting, for it rises between the horns of Shaytaan."*

There are certain times when it is disliked to perform any type of Salah. Our Prophet ﷺ has prevented us from performing Salah at these times:

1. From the start of sunrise up until the sun has fully risen i.e. approximately 30 minutes immediately after sunrise.

2. During midday, when the sun is at its highest (Zawaal).

3. Approximately 20 minutes immediately before sunset up until sunset, unless one has yet to perform Asr Salah.

4. These times differ depending on location and time of the year.

Sun is at its highest point (Zawaal)

Times when performing Salah is disliked

10 mins before and 10 mins after Midday

Approximately 30 Minutes after sunrise

20 minutes before sunset up until sunset

Sunrise

Sunset

THE DAILY PRAYERS

فجر	ظهر	عصر	مغرب	عشاء
2 Sunnah	4 Sunnah	4 Sunnah	3 Fardh	4 Sunnah
2 Fardh	4 Fardh	4 Fardh	2 Sunnah	4 Fardh
	2 Sunnah		2 Nafl	2 Sunnah
	2 Nafl			2 Nafl
				3 Witr
				2 Nafl

Fardh	Fardh is the most important type of action which must be performed. If one leaves it out, they will be a major sinner.
Wajib	Wajib is almost as important as a Fardh act and our Prophet ﷺ never left it out. It is a sin to leave a Wajib act.
Sunnah Muakkadah	Literally means "Emphasised Sunnah" which must be performed. It is a sin to leave out a Sunnah Muakkadah without a valid reason.
Sunnah Ghayr Muakkadah	Literally means a "Non-emphasised Sunnah". Leaving out a Sunnah Ghayr Muakkadah is not a sin. There is great emphasis on performing all types of Sunnah and there are great rewards for adhering to the Sunnah. The greatest of which is closeness to our Prophet ﷺ.
Nafl	Is an action that brings us reward if we perform it.

EXERCISE FIVE

FOR EACH SALAH, INDICATE WHEN THE TIME BEGINS AND ENDS FOR TODAY'S DATE.
(IN HOURS AND MINUTES)

Date: __ / __ / ____

	Beginning time	Ending time	
Fajr			فجر
Dhuhr			ظهر
Asr			عصر
Maghrib			مغرب
Isha			عشاء

LESSON SIX-SALAH

To ensure Salah is performed correctly, we must fulfil certain conditions before we begin. They are necessary and must not be left out. If a condition of the prayer is not fulfilled, intentionally or unintentionally, the prayer will be invalid.

The conditions of Salah are:

1. **Taharah (Purity):** The body, clothes and the place where Salah is to be performed must be pure from all minor and major impurities.

2. **Satr Al-Awrah (Covering the body):** Certain parts of the body must be covered for Salah to be valid. The Awrah for a man is to cover the body from the navel up until the knees. The Awrah for a woman is to cover the entire body except for the face, hands and feet.

3. **Istiqbaal Al-Qiblah (Facing the Qiblah):** Face the Qiblah when performing Salah. The Qiblah (direction) is the Ka'bah in Makkah Al-Mukarramah. If the Qiblah (direction) is unclear, an attempt must be made to estimate the direction.

4. **Waqt (Time):** Each Salah must be performed at its correct time. If any Salah is performed before or after its time, it will not be valid. One must be certain that they are performing the prayer within the time of that prayer for it to be valid.

5. **Niyyah (Intention):** Have firm intention in the heart before performing Salah.

6. **Takbeer Tahreema (The opening Takbeer):** Recite اَللهُ أَكْبَرُ when starting Salah.

FARDH ACTS OF SALAH

There are 7 Faraidh of Salah. They are obligatory. If any one of these actions are missed, Salah will not be valid and must be repeated.

The Faraidh acts of Salah are:

1. **Takbeer Tahreema (Opening Takbeer):** The opening Takbeer when starting Salah.

2. **Qiyaam (Standing):** This is obligatory in Fardh and Wajib prayers for someone who is able to stand. However, Fardh and Wajib prayers can be performed whilst sitting if there is a valid reason to do so. For example, if someone has a broken leg and is unable to stand up.

3. **Qira'ah (Recitation):** Recite at least one long verse (Ayah) or three short Ayahs from the Qur'aan in the first two Raka'ahs of any Fardh Salah and in all Raka'ahs of Witr, Sunnah and Nafl Salah.

4. **Ruku' (Bowing):** Bow in every Raka'ah of prayer in such a manner that the hands reach the knees.

5. **Sajdah (Prostration):** Prostrate twice in every Raka'ah of prayer.

6. **Qa'dah Akheerah (Last sitting):** The sitting at the end of the final Raka'ah.

7. **Khurooj-Bi-Sun'ihi (Ending the prayer):** End the prayer with an action such as the Salaam.

MODEL PRAYER

Raka'ah 1

Takbeer Tahreema
- Face Qiblah
- Make Niyyah
- Say اَللهُ اَكْبَرُ raising the hands up to the ears

Qiyaam
- Recite Thana
- Recite Ta'awwudh
- Recite Tasmiyah
- Recite Al-Fatiha
- Recite any Surah

Ruku'
- Say اَللهُ اَكْبَرُ whilst going into Ruku'
- Recite 3 times سُبْحَانَ رَبِّيَ الْعَظِيْمِ

Qawmah
- As you stand up recite سَمِعَ اللهُ لِمَنْ حَمِدَهُ
- Whilst standing recite رَبَّنَا وَلَكَ الْحَمْدُ

Raka'ah 2

Qiyam
- Recite Tasmiyah
- Recite Al-Fatiha
- Recite any Surah

Ruku'
- Say اَللهُ اَكْبَرُ whilst going into Ruku'
- Recite 3 times سُبْحَانَ رَبِّيَ الْعَظِيْمِ

Qawmah
- As you stand up recite سَمِعَ اللهُ لِمَنْ حَمِدَهُ
- Whilst standing recite رَبَّنَا وَلَكَ الْحَمْدُ

1st Sajdah
- Say اَللهُ اَكْبَرُ whilst going into Sajdah
- Recite 3 times سُبْحَانَ رَبِّيَ الْأَعْلَى

Raka'ah 3

Qiyam
- Recite Tasmiyah
- Recite Al-Fatiha
- Recite any Surah

Ruku'
- Say اَللهُ اَكْبَرُ whilst going into Ruku'
- Recite 3 times سُبْحَانَ رَبِّيَ الْعَظِيْمِ

Qawmah
- As you stand up recite سَمِعَ اللهُ لِمَنْ حَمِدَهُ
- Whilst standing recite رَبَّنَا وَلَكَ الْحَمْدُ

1st Sajdah
- Say اَللهُ اَكْبَرُ whilst going into Sajdah
- Recite 3 times سُبْحَانَ رَبِّيَ الْأَعْلَى

Raka'ah 4

Qiyam
- Recite Tasmiyah
- Recite Al-Fatiha
- Recite any Surah

Ruku'
- Say اَللهُ اَكْبَرُ whilst going into Ruku'
- Recite 3 times سُبْحَانَ رَبِّيَ الْعَظِيْمِ

Qawmah
- As you stand up recite سَمِعَ اللهُ لِمَنْ حَمِدَهُ
- Whilst standing recite رَبَّنَا وَلَكَ الْحَمْدُ

1st Sajdah
- Say اَللهُ اَكْبَرُ whilst going into Sajdah
- Recite 3 times سُبْحَانَ رَبِّيَ الْأَعْلَى

1st Sajdah
- Say اَللهُ اَكْبَرُ whilst going into Sajdah
- Recite 3 times سُبْحَانَ رَبِّيَ الْأَعْلَى

Jalsah
- Say اَللهُ اَكْبَرُ and sit up

2nd Sajdah
- Say اَللهُ اَكْبَرُ whilst going into second Sajdah
- Recite 3 times سُبْحَانَ رَبِّيَ الْأَعْلَى

Jalsah
- Say اَللهُ اَكْبَرُ and sit up

2nd Sajdah
- Say اَللهُ اَكْبَرُ whilst going into second Sajdah
- Recite 3 times سُبْحَانَ رَبِّيَ الْأَعْلَى

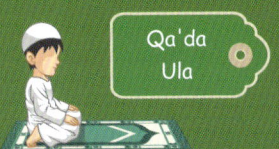

Qa'da Ula
- Recite Tashahhud
- Stand up saying اَللهُ اَكْبَرُ

Jalsah
- Say اَللهُ اَكْبَرُ and sit up

2nd Sajdah
- Say اَللهُ اَكْبَرُ whilst going into second Sajdah
- Recite 3 times سُبْحَانَ رَبِّيَ الْأَعْلَى

> Note: In Fardh Salah there is no need to pray a Surah in the third and fourth Raka'ah after reciting Surah Al-Fatiha.

Jalsah
- Say اَللهُ اَكْبَرُ and sit up

2nd Sajdah
- Say اَللهُ اَكْبَرُ whilst going into second Sajdah
- Recite 3 times سُبْحَانَ رَبِّيَ الْأَعْلَى

Qa'da Akheera
- Recite Tashahhud
- Recite Durood Ibrahimi
- Recite Duaa

Khurooj Bi Sunihi
- Finish the Salah by reciting السَّلَامُ عَلَيْكُمْ وَرَحْمَةُ اللهِ turning your head towards the right shoulder then again, the same towards the left shoulder.

WAJIB ACTS OF SALAH

Wajib acts are those which are necessary to perform during Salah. If a Wajib act is left out intentionally, the prayer will need to be repeated. However, if left out unintentionally a prostration of forgetfulness (Sajdah Al-Sahw) is necessary.

The Wajib acts in Salah can be divided into 4 categories:

2 Wajibaat for the whole Salah:

1. Perform every act of Salah in order.
2. Perform every act of Salah in a calm manner.

5 Wajibaat of Qira'ah:

1. Recite Surah Al-Fatiha.
2. Recite Surah Al-Fatiha before any other Surah.
3. Recite at least one long Ayah or 3 short Ayaat from the Qur'an in the first 2 Raka'ahs of any Fardh Salah.
4. Recite at least one long Ayah or 3 short Ayaat from the Qur'an in all Raka'ahs of Wajib, Sunnah and Nafl Salah.
5. The Imaam must recite aloud in Fajr, Jumu'ah, Taraweeh, Witr in Ramadaan, Eid Salah and the first 2 Raka'ahs of Maghrib and Isha Salah. The Imaam must recite quietly in Dhuhr and Asr.

5 Wajibaat from Qawmah to Salaam:

1. Stand in Qawmah (the standing position after Ruku'').

2. Sit in Jalsah (the sitting position between the two Sajdahs).

3. Sit in Qa'dah Ula.

4. Recite Tashahhud in each Qa'dah.

5. End the Salah with السَّلاَمُ عَلَيْكُمْ وَرَحْمَةُ الله

1 additional Wajib for Witr Salah only:

Witr is a Wajib Salah and is performed as three Raka'ah with one Salam at the end of the three Raka'ah. In the first two Raka'ah, Salah is performed as normal and in the third Raka'ah perform an extra Takbeer after reciting Surah Al-Fatiha and another Surah. Then recite Duaa Al-Qunoot. The remainder of the Salah is completed as normal.

SUNNAH ACTS IN SALAH FOR A MUNFARID (PRAYING ALONE)

Sunnah acts of Qiyaam:
- Raising both hands up to the ears with the palms facing the Qiblah when reciting Takbeer Tahreema. Females should raise their hands up to their shoulders only.
- Grasping the wrist of your left arm with your right hand and holding it below the navel. Women should place their hands on their chest.

Sunnah acts of Recitation:
- Reciting Thana quietly after Takbeer Tahreema.
- Reciting Ta'awwudh at the start of the first Raka'ah.
- Reciting Tasmiyah before reciting Surah Al-Fatiha and any other Surah.
- In the 3rd and 4th Raka'ah of a Fardh Salah, only reciting Surah Al-Fatiha.
- Saying Ameen quietly after the recitation of Surah Al-Fatiha.

Sunnah acts of Ruku' and Sujood:
- When performing Ruku', keeping the back and head in line.
- During Ruku', grasping the knees firmly with both hands whilst keeping the fingers spread. Women should not spread their fingers.
- Reciting the Tasbeeh for Ruku' and Sujood at least 3 times.
- When returning to the Qawmah position, reciting Tasmee' سَمِعَ اللهُ لِمَنْ حَمِدَهُ and Tahmeed رَبَّنَا وَ لَكَ الْحَمْدُ
- When going into Sujood, placing the knees on the ground first, followed by the hands, the nose and finally the forehead.

- In Sujood, keeping the arms separate from the side of the body, the stomach separate from the thighs and not resting the arms on the ground. A female should join her arms with her sides and her stomach with her thighs. She should also join the back of her thighs with her calves and her shins should be placed on the ground.

Sunnah acts of Qa'dah and Jalsa
- In Qa'dah or Jalsa, placing the left foot on the ground horizontally and sitting on it whilst keeping the right foot raised with the toes facing the Qiblah. A female should sit on her bottom with both feet extended towards the right.
- Raising the index finger when reciting Tashahhud.
- Reciting Al-Salat-Ul-Ibrahimi after Tashahhud.
- Reciting a Duaa after Al-Salat-Al-Ibrahimi.

If a Sunnah act is missed in Salah, Salah is still valid. However, if these Sunnah acts are performed in Salah, the reward for the Salah will be increased.

EXERCISE SIX

FROM THE LIST OF SALAH ACTIONS BELOW PLACE EACH ACT IN ITS CORRECT BOX.

Purity	Qiyaam	Qira'ah	Intention	Tasbeeh x3
Face Qiblah	Performing acts in order	Sajdah	Reciting Surah Fatiha	Thana
Reciting Tashahhud	Duaa Qunoot	Covering the body	Jalsah	Tasmiyah
Ending with Salam	Time of prayer	Qa'dah Akheera	Qawmah	Back and head in line
Ruku'	Khurooj Bi Sunihi	Qa'dah Ula	Al-Salat-ul-Ibrahimi	Hands below the navel

Fardh	Wajib	Conditions	Sunnah

FILL IN THE BLANKS BELOW.

1. The_____ and _____ must be pure before performing Salah.

2. To face the direction of the_____ is a condition of_____.

3. Takbeer Tahreema is when we recite_____ at the beginning of Salah.

4. It is Sunnah to raise the finger when reciting _____.

Answer the following

1. Ibrahim was performing Fajr Salah. After he had completed Salah he realised that it was not yet time for Fajr.

Is Ibrahim's Salah valid and does he need to anything more?

_____
_____
_____

2. Fareed realised after completing Dhuhr Salah that he did not recite a Surah of the Qur'aan in his 2nd Raka'ah. He also remembered he did not sit in Qa'dah Ula.

Is his Salah valid and does he need to do anything more?

_____
_____
_____

LESSON SEVEN-BREAKERS AND MAKROOH ACTS OF SALAH

Makrooh acts are those which are disliked or offensive. If a Makrooh act is performed during Salah, one's Salah is still valid but the reward for performing the Salah will be reduced.

Here is a list of some actions which are Makrooh:

- Fidgeting with the clothes or the body.
- Straightening your clothes, for example to lift the trousers when going into Sajdah.
- Cracking the knuckles.
- Stretching out.
- Yawning (you should try to suppress it).
- Closing the eyes.
- Performing Salah whilst having the urge to relieve yourself or to release wind.
- Moving the head and looking around.
- Coughing without any reason.
- Performing Salah wearing clothes with pictures of living objects on them.
- Praying alone in a row when there is space in the row in front in Jama'ah.

ACTS THAT BREAK SALAH

There are certain acts that break Salah.

- Eating or drinking whilst performing Salah.
- Talking in Salah knowingly or unknowingly, even if it is a few words.
- Greeting a person whilst performing Salah.
- Replying to greetings.
- Replying to a sneeze saying Yar'HamukAllah يَرْحَمُكَ اللهُ.
- Laughing aloud during Salah.
  (This also breaks the Wudhu)
- Making any unnecessary noise.
- Turning the chest away from the Qiblah.
- Reciting the Qur'aan by looking at the text.
- Stepping ahead of the Imaam during Salah.
- Excessive movement during Salah which may make it appear to an onlooker as though one is not in Salah.

EXERCISE SEVEN

ANSWER THE QUESTIONS BELOW.

1. There are many acts that are Makrooh when performing Salah. List five acts in Salah that are Makrooh.

_____   _____

_____   _____

_____

2. State five acts that would break one's Salah.

_____   _____

_____   _____

_____

3. Explain the consequence of performing a Makrooh action during Salah.

_____

_____

_____

4. Kareem has reached the mosque late for Isha Salah. When he gets there, he decides to pray alone in a row by himself rather than join in the spaces in the row ahead.

Is Kareem right to do this? Explain your answer.

_____

_____

_____

5. Jaabir is praying the Sunnah of Asr Salah in the Masjid. Ahmed is doing the same behind him. Ahmed sees that Jaabir is wearing shorts that are above his knees, and this causes Ahmed to laugh out loud. After they have both completed Salah, Jabir asks Ahmed why he laughed and Ahmed explained to him why.

Explain whether Ahmed's Salah is valid or not and identify any further acts that Ahmed must perform.

_____
_____
_____
_____
_____
_____
_____

Explain whether Jabir's Salah is valid or not and identify any further that acts Jabir must perform.

_____
_____
_____
_____
_____
_____
_____

LESSON EIGHT - SAJDAH AL-SAHW

If one or more of the Wajib acts of Salah are left out forgetfully, it becomes Wajib to perform Sajdah Al-Sahw (prostration of forgetfulness). By performing Sajdah Al-Sahw, the Salah is valid. If one does not perform Sajdah Al-Sahw, the Salah must be repeated.

If a Fardh act of Salah has been missed intentionally or unintentionally, the Salah must be repeated. Sajdah Sahw cannot be used to compensate a Fardh act.

Sajdah Sahw becomes Wajib when one of the following happens:

1. Any Wajib act of Salah is missed out unintentionally, such as forgetting to recite Surah Al-Fatiha.
2. Any Wajib act of Salah is delayed.
3. The order of any Wajib act in Salah is changed, such as reciting a Surah before Surah Al-Fatiha.

How to perform Sajdah Al-Sahw

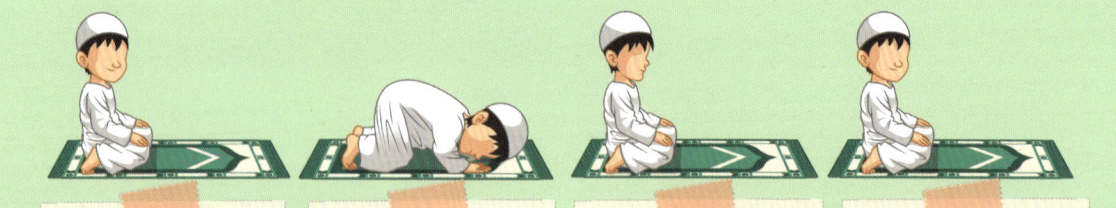

In the final Raka'ah after reciting Tashahhud, perform a single Salaam to the right side only.

Thereafter, perform two Sujood reciting the Tasbeeh of Sajdah in each of them.

After making the two Sujood, recite Tashahhud, Al-Salat-ul-Ibrahimi and Duaa.

Finally, perform Salaam as normal to end the prayer.

CONGREGATIONAL PRAYER (JAMA'AH)

> وَارْكَعُوْا مَعَ الرَّاكِعِيْنَ
>
> "And bow your head with those who bow in worship"
> Surah Al-Baqarah, Ayah No: 43

It is Wajib to perform Salah in congregation (Jama'ah). A single Salah performed with Jama'ah has 27 times more reward than a Salah performed on its own. Jama'ah is Wajib for males and to miss it even once without a reason is a sin.

A Jama'ah is fulfilled when there is an Imaam and at least one Muqtadee. It can be performed in a mosque or at home, although Jama'ah in a mosque is best.

It is from the Sunnah that the most knowledgeable person on the rules of Salah or the best in reciting the Qur'aan should lead the prayer. It is also from the Sunnah that the rows should be straight without any gaps between the people praying. It is recommended that the Imaam instructs the people to straighten the rows, leaving no gaps and standing shoulder to shoulder.

You should not think 'I can't make it for Jama'ah, I am too busy with school or work and family', because this thought is from Shaytaan. If you make the intention and effort, إِنْشَاءَاللّٰه Allah ﷻ will make it easy.

EXERCISE EIGHT

ANSWER THE QUESTIONS BELOW.

1. Ali is learning his prayer and is confused on what to do when he makes a mistake. He assumes that he needs to do a prostration at the end of the prayer whenever he misses anything out of his prayer.

a) When is a prostration of forgetfulness required?

_____
_____
_____

b) Mention three acts that would require a prostration of forgetfulness and mention three that would not.

_____   _____
_____   _____
_____   _____

c) Describe how Ali should perform a prostration of forgetfulness.

_____
_____
_____
_____
_____
_____

2. Burhaan is praying behind Zahid who stands up for the third Raka'ah without having sat for Qa'dah Ula. Burhaan stays sitting waiting for Zahid to sit back down.

a) What is Zahid required to do in the following two cases:

Zahid has lifted his knees off the ground but is not yet standing

_____
_____
_____

Zahid has stood all the way up

_____
_____
_____

b) What happens to the prayer if Zahid had done the same thing after the fourth Raka'ah and had stood up for the fifth Raka'ah?

_____
_____
_____
_____

LESSON NINE - PRAYER OF A MASBOOQ

Here are some important terms to be aware of:

1. Imaam (The one who leads Salah)
2. Muqtadee (The one following the Imaam)
3. Munfarid (The one who prays on his own)
4. Masbooq (The latecomer to the prayer who has missed at least one Raka'ah)

If one attends the Jama'ah and is late in joining, it is necessary to join the prayer regardless of how many Raka'ahs have been missed. The Masbooq (latecomer) makes up any Raka'ahs that he has missed in their original order.

A Raka'ah has been missed if the Masbooq joins after the Imaam has stood up from Ruku'.

- If the Imaam is in Ruku', the Muqtadee must recite the Takbeer and join the Imaam in the Ruku' position.
- If you join the Salah after the Imaam has stood up from Ruku', then that Raka'ah has been missed.
- If the Imaam is in the Jalsah position in the 2nd or 4th Raka'ah, the Masbooq should recite the Takbeer and join the Imaam in Jalsah straight away.

Once the Imaam has completed the Salah, you should then stand and make up the Raka'aat that you have missed.

Raka'aat missed	Raka'aat with Imaam	How to complete the prayer
1	3	Stand up after the Imaam has completed the Salah. Recite: • Thana, Ta'awwudh and Tasmiyah. • Surah Fatiha and a Surah. Finish the rest of the Raka'ah. After the Sajdah, sit and recite Tashahhud, Al-Salat-ul-Ibrahimi, Duaa and complete the Salah.
2	2	Stand up after the Imaam has completed the Salah. Recite: • Thana, Ta'awwudh and Tasmiyah. • Surah Fatiha and a Surah. Stand up for the last Raka'ah after Sajdah. Recite: • Tasmiyah, Surah Al-Fatiha and a Surah. Sit after Sajdah and complete Salah as normal.
3	1	Stand up after the Imaam has performed Salaam. Recite: • Thana, Ta'awwudh and Tasmiyah. • Surah Al-Fatiha and a Surah. Sit down after Sajdah and recite Tashahhud only, then stand up for the next Raka'ah. Recite: • Tasmiyah, Surah Al-Fatiha and a Surah. Do not sit down after the Sajdah but stand straight up for the last Raka'ah. Recite: • Tasmiyah and Surah Al-Fatiha After the Sajdah, sit and complete Salah as normal.
4	0	Stand up after the Imaam has performed Salaam and pray as you are performing 4 Raka'ah Salah alone.

What to do if you have missed one or more Raka'aat in Maghrib Salah.

Raka'aat missed	Raka'aat with Imaam	How to complete the prayer
1	2	Stand up after the Imaam has performed Salaam. Recite: • Thana, Ta'awwudh and Tasmiyah. • Surah Al-Fatiha and a Surah. Finish the rest of the Raka'ah. After the Sajdah, sit and recite Tashahhud, Al-Salat-ul-Ibrahimi and Duaa.
2	1	Stand up after the Imam has performed Salaam. Recite: • Thana, Ta'awwudh and Tasmiyah. • Surah Fatiha and a Surah. Sit down after Sajdah and recite Tashahhud only, then stand up for the next Raka'ah. Recite: • Tasmiyah, Surah Al-Fatiha and a Surah. After the Sajdah, sit and complete Salah as normal.
3	0	Stand up after the Imam has performed Salaam and pray as you are praying 3 Raka'ah Salah alone.

EXERCISE NINE

ANSWER THE QUESTIONS BELOW.

1. After the completion of which act within the Raka'ah has the latecomer missed the Raka'ah?

___

2. Paddy arrives late for the Asr prayer. When he reaches the prayer hall, he realises that the Imaam is in the Qiyaam position in the second Raka'ah. He quickly joins the congregation.

a. How many Raka'ahs has Paddy missed?

___

b. Once the Imaam has completed the prayer, what does Paddy need to do to complete his prayer?

___

3. Paddy again arrives late for the Maghrib congregation. He joins the Imaam in congregation whilst the Imaam is in the Qiyaam position of the third Raka'ah. Once the Imaam has finished the prayer, how should Paddy complete his prayer?

___

LESSON TEN - THE DAY OF JUMU'AH

Friday is the day of Jumu'ah. It is a day when people gather to perform Jumu'ah Salah in congregation. A person who misses Jumu'ah Salah without a valid reason is a sinner. Those people who miss Jumu'ah Salah due to illness or any other reason must perform Dhuhr Salah instead. The time of Jumu'ah Salah begins immediately after Zawaal and ends when the time of Dhuhr concludes.

The Sunnahs of Jumúah

- Dua
- Surah Al-Kahf
- Bathe
- Miswaak
- Trim nails
- Go to the Mosque early
- Salawaat
- Clean clothes

Preferred method of Jumu'ah Salah

- Adhaan
- 4 Raka'ah Sunnah Mu'akkadah.
- 2nd Adhaan.
- 2 Khutbahs (sermons).
- 2 Fardh Raka'ah of Jumu'ah (Perform in congregation)
- 4 Raka'ah Sunnah Mu'akkadah.
- 2 Raka'ah Sunnah Mu'akkadah.
- 2 Raka'ah Nafl.

The two Khutbahs (sermons) must be delivered in Arabic with a short interval of sitting by the Khateeb (person delivering the Khutbah) between the two.

It is not permissible to do the following whilst the Khutbah is being delivered:

Greeting	Talking	Using a phone
Eating	Loud Dhikr or Duaa	Praying

LESSON ELEVEN - FASTING (اَلصَّوْمُ)

> **SAWM (FASTING) MEANS TO ABSTAIN FROM EATING, DRINKING AND MARITAL RELATIONS FROM THE BREAK OF DAWN UNTIL SUNSET. IT IS AN ACT WHICH IS CARRIED OUT DURING THE MONTH OF RAMADAAN AND IS ONE OF THE PILLARS OF ISLAM.**

Sayyiduna Sahl ؓ narrates that the Prophet Muhammad ﷺ said, "In Paradise, there is a gate called Al-Rayyaan, through which those who used to fast will enter and no one but they will enter it. It will be said, 'Where are those who fasted?' They will rise and none will enter it but them. When they have entered, it will be locked and no one else will enter." (Al-Bukhari)

It is Fardh upon every Muslim, who is of mature age and sane mind, to fast in Ramadaan. Fasting brings one closer to Allah ﷻ. Fasting has many physical, moral and spiritual benefits.

There are different types of fasts:

Fardh
Fasting in the holy month of Ramadaan..

Mustahab
- 6 days in the month of Shawwal.
- First eight days of Dhul Hijjah.
- Every Monday and Thursday.

Sunnah
- The Day of Arafah (9th Dhul Hijjah).
- The Day of Ashurah (10th Muharram).
- The 13th, 14th and 15th days of every Islamic month.

Makrooh Tahrimi
- 5 Days of the year: Eid ul-Fitr, Eid ul-Adha and 3 days after Eid ul-Adha (11th, 12th and 13th Dhul Hijjah).

Important terms

Qadaa: Making up a missed fast.

Kaffarah: Keeping 60 fasts consecutively for a fast that was broken intentionally.

What breaks a fast?

Actions which break a fast are of two types:

1. An action that breaks the fast making only Qadaa necessary. For example, eating after subh sadiq (dawn) believing that the time for Fajr has not yet begun.

2. An action that breaks the fast making Qadaa and Kaffarah necessary. For example, eating deliberately during the day.

If one is unable to fast for 60 days consecutively, there are 3 alternatives:

1. To feed 60 poor people two full meals.

2. If one is unable to complete the first, then feed 1 poor person 2 full meals for 60 days.

3. If one is unable to complete either of the above then one must give the equivalent of 2 full meals in cash to charity.

Duaa for beginning the fast

اَللّٰهُمَّ اَصُوْمُ غَدًا لَّكَ فَاغْفِرْ لِيْ مَا قَدَّمْتُ وَمَا آخَّرْتُ

Duaa for ending the fast

اَللّٰهُمَّ اِنِّیْ لَكَ صُمْتُ وَبِكَ اٰمَنْتُ وَعَلَیْكَ تَوَكَّلْتُ وَعَلٰی رِزْقِكَ اَفْطَرْتُ فَتَقَبَّلْ مِنِّیْ

Acts that break the fast for which Qadaa is required
- To eat and drink after Subh Sadiq (Dawn) believing that the fast has not yet begun or to eat before sunset thinking that the fast has ended.
- If water unintentionally goes down the throat e.g. when gargling.
- Intentionally vomiting a mouthful or swallowing vomit.
- Swallowing the blood from gums when the colour of the blood is more than the saliva with which it is mixed.
- Intentionally swallowing an item which is not food.
- Using an inhaler for medicinal purposes.

Acts that break the fast for which both Qadaa and Kaffarah are Wajib
To complete any action which breaks the fast intentionally. For example, to eat or drink deliberately without a valid reason.

Mustahab acts in fasting
- Eating and drinking at Suhoor (meal before Subh Sadiq).
- Ending a fast immediately after Sunset.
- Ending a fast with dates. If dates are not available, one should end a fast with water.
- Make the intention to fast in the night before beginning the fast.

Actions which *do not* break the fast

ONE
Applying perfume (ltr)

TWO
Eating or drinking forgetting one is fasting

THREE
Water entering the ears

FOUR
Swallowing saliva

FIVE
Vomiting unintentionally or vomiting less than a mouthful intentionally

SIX
Nose Bleed

SEVEN
Using a Miswak

And many more...

EXERCISE ELEVEN

ANSWER THE QUESTIONS BELOW.

1. What is fasting (saum)?
   _____
   _____

2. a. It is Fardh to fast in _____
   b. It is Sunnah to fast on _____
   c. It is Mustahab to fast on _____
   d. It is Haraam to fast on _____

3. List three actions which would break the fast
   _____
   _____

4. List three actions which would not break the fast
   _____
   _____

5. Explain the following:

Qadaa fast
_____
_____

Kaffarah
_____
_____

6. In what situation is: a. Qadaa necessary? b. Kaffarah necessary? Provide an example of each one.

_____
_____
_____
_____
_____

7. Muhammad was at school one day. During class his friend Sam was handing out sweets to the entire class in celebration of his birthday. Muhammad was fasting that day but he had forgotten he was fasting. He took some sweets and ate them. After a short time, he realised the mistake he had made and was extremely concerned about what he had done.

What is the ruling in this situation and what does Muhammad need to do?

_____
_____
_____
_____

If Muhammad had eaten the sweets intentionally, knowing that he was fasting, what would be the ruling and what would Muhammad need to do?

_____
_____
_____
_____
_____

LESSON TWELVE-HAJJ (THE PILGRIMAGE)

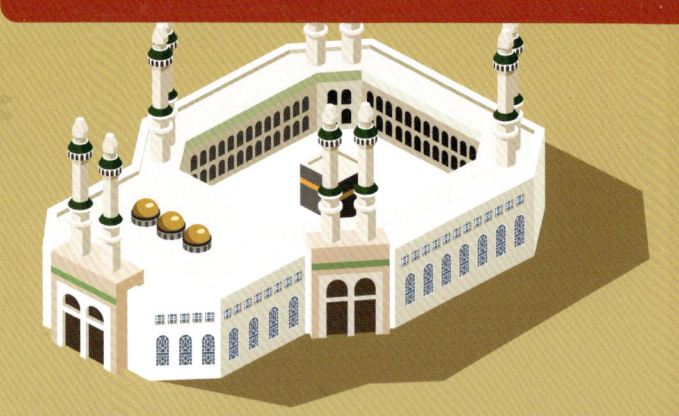

Hajj is the fifth pillar of Islam. It is compulsory upon every adult to perform Hajj once in a lifetime if the following conditions are met:

- If they have enough money for the journey.
- If they are in good health.

The Messenger of Allah ﷺ said, "He who makes pilgrimage to the house, avoiding indecent and immoral behaviour, will return purified from sins like the day he was born." (Al-Bukhari)

The features of Hajj are as follows:

- Ihraam: The two pieces of unsewn white cloth worn by a male covering the entire body except for the feet and head. A female should cover everything except for her face using normal clothing such as an abaya.
- 2 Raka'ahs of Prayer: This prayer should be performed after wearing the Ihraam.
- Intention (Niyyah): Having a firm intention to perform Hajj.
- Reciting Talbiyah: (Labayk)

- Tawaaf: Circumambulate the Ka'bah seven times upon arrival in Makkah Al-Mukarramah.
- Sa'ee: Walking seven times between the hills of Safa and Marwah.
- Spending the night of the 8th of Dhul-Hijjah in Mina.
- Staying in Arafah on the 9th of Dhul-Hijjah.
- Spending the night of 9th of Dhul-Hijjah in Muzdalifah.

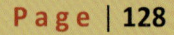

The steps of Hajj

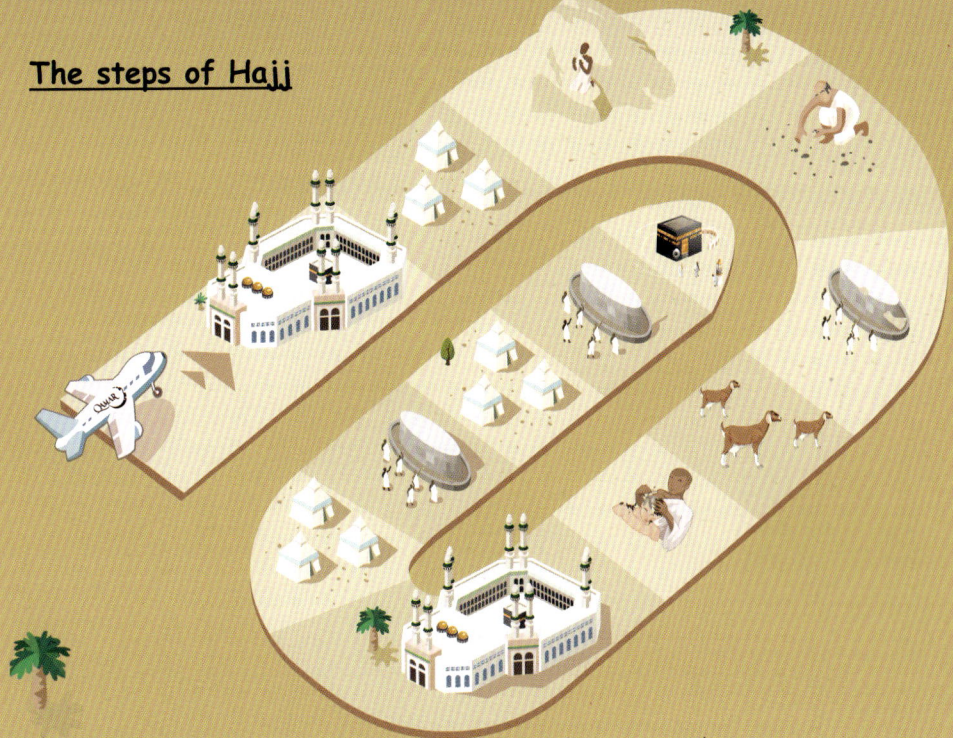

- Stoning the Jamarat Al-Aqaba in Mina on the 10th of Dhul-Hijjah.
- Sacrificing an animal in Mina.
- Shaving or trimming of the hair of the head.
- Tawaaf Al-Ifadhah: Performing Tawaaf around the Ka'bah and performing Sa'ee.
- Stoning all 3 pillars in Mina, on the 11th and 12th of Dhul-Hijjah.
- Tawaaf Al-Wada (Farewell Tawaaf): Performing Tawaaf around the Ka'bah.

When one goes to Makkah Al-Mukarramah to perform Umrah or Hajj, they should also visit Al-Madinah Al-Munawwarah. Our Prophet Muhammad ﷺ is resting here in Al-Masjid Al-Nabawi so we should go and visit him.

Note: If a child performs Hajj and they are not of mature age then Hajj must be completed again when they are of mature age.

Page | 129

EXERCISE TWELVE

ANSWER THE QUESTIONS BELOW.

1. What is Hajj?
___
___
___
___

2. What two conditions must be met in order for Hajj to be compulsory upon a Muslim?
___
___

3. List the 15 features of Hajj below.
___
___
___
___
___
___
___
___
___
___
___
___
___
___
___

4. What did our Prophet ﷺ advise us regarding the reward of performing Hajj?

___

5. Kareem performed Hajj with his father when he was 3 years old. He is now 17 years of age. Is Hajj compulsory for him to perform or did the Hajj he performed as a child fulfil his obligation? Explain your answer.

___

Qamar Learning Academy

اَلسِّيرَة

What's in this section?

QURAYSH MEET AT DAR AL-NADWAH
- The evil plot
- Allah's ﷻ plan for Rasoolullah ﷺ

THE HIJRAH

ARRIVAL IN AL-MADINAH AL-MUNAWWARAH
- Awaiting the beloved
- The full moon rises

BUILDING OF THE MASJID
- The mosque of Rasoolullah ﷺ
- Building the bonds of brotherhood
- Bringing peace to Al-Madinah
- The hypocrites
- The call to prayer

THE CUSP OF WAR
- Abdullah Ibn Jahsh ﷺ & his mission
- The muslim army rises
- The battlefield of Badr
- Allah ﷻ helps the believers

BATTLE OF UHUD
- Consulting the companions
- Hypocrites desert the Muslims
- The Archers' dilemma
- The aftermath
- Uhud Illustrated

BATTLE OF AL-AHZAAB
- The Alliance
- The arrival of the enemy
- Overcoming adversity

RASOOLULLAH'S ﷺ BLESSED LINEAGE

THE BEAUTY OF HIS ﷺ BLESSED FORM
- Belongings of Rasoolullah ﷺ

SEERAH

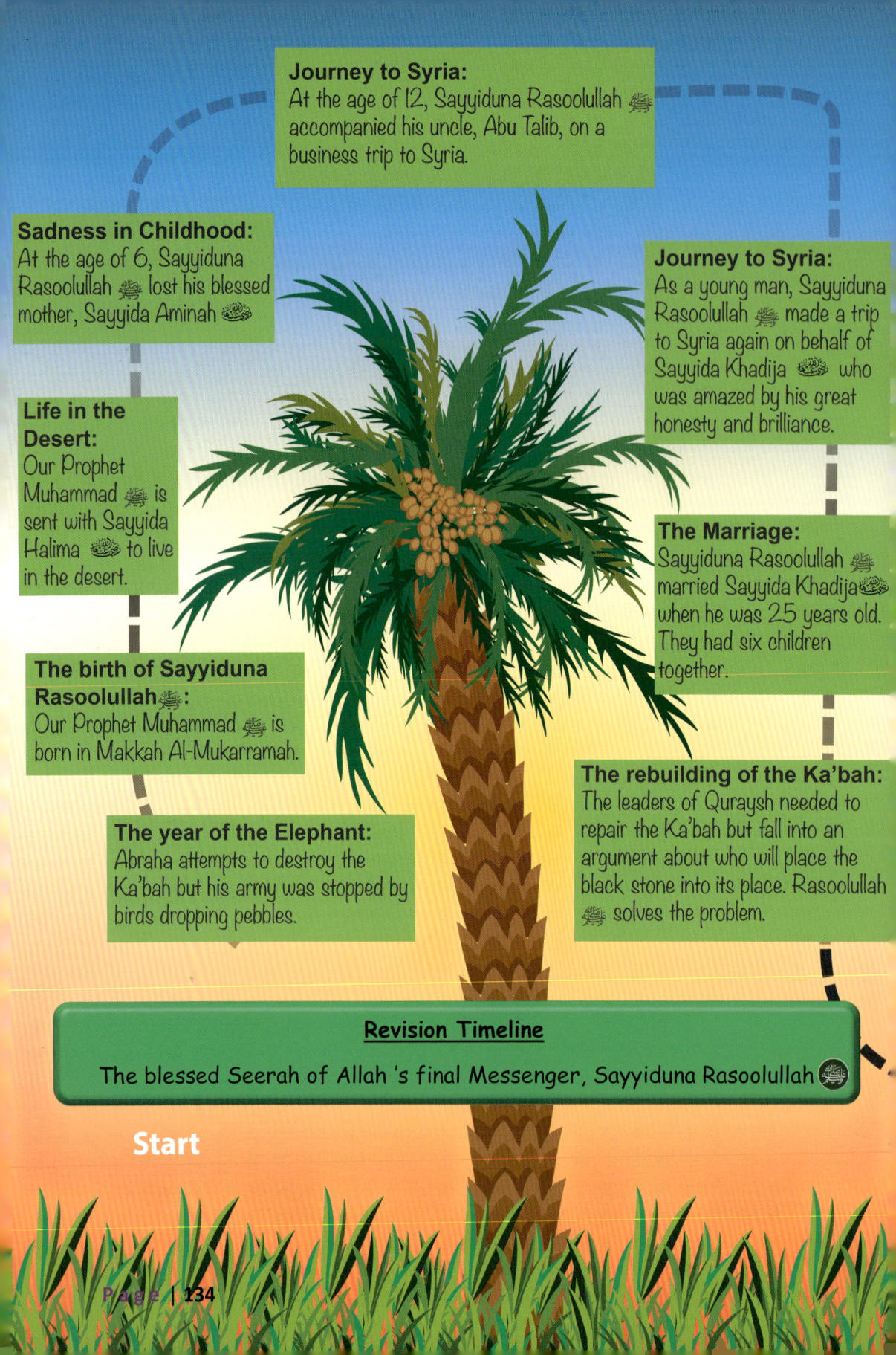

Journey to Syria:
At the age of 12, Sayyiduna Rasoolullah ﷺ accompanied his uncle, Abu Talib, on a business trip to Syria.

Sadness in Childhood:
At the age of 6, Sayyiduna Rasoolullah ﷺ lost his blessed mother, Sayyida Aminah ؓ

Journey to Syria:
As a young man, Sayyiduna Rasoolullah ﷺ made a trip to Syria again on behalf of Sayyida Khadija ؓ who was amazed by his great honesty and brilliance.

Life in the Desert:
Our Prophet Muhammad ﷺ is sent with Sayyida Halima ؓ to live in the desert.

The Marriage:
Sayyiduna Rasoolullah ﷺ married Sayyida Khadija ؓ when he was 25 years old. They had six children together.

The birth of Sayyiduna Rasoolullah ﷺ:
Our Prophet Muhammad ﷺ is born in Makkah Al-Mukarramah.

The year of the Elephant:
Abraha attempts to destroy the Ka'bah but his army was stopped by birds dropping pebbles.

The rebuilding of the Ka'bah:
The leaders of Quraysh needed to repair the Ka'bah but fall into an argument about who will place the black stone into its place. Rasoolullah ﷺ solves the problem.

Revision Timeline
The blessed Seerah of Allah's final Messenger, Sayyiduna Rasoolullah ﷺ

Start

Migration to Abyssinia: Some of the Muslims were granted permission to migrate to the land of Abyssinia, in Africa. Here they were able to practice Islam freely.

The Year of Sorrow: Sayyiduna Rasoolullah ﷺ lost both his beloved uncle Abu Talib and his beloved wife, the mother of the believers, Sayyida Khadija ؓ.

Torture & Persecution: The Makkans started to persecute the Muslims in Makkah. Many were tortured and beaten regularly. The Quraysh refused to allow the Muslims to practice their religion.

Al-Isra & Al-Me'raj: Sayyiduna Rasoolullah ﷺ undertook a miraculous night journey from Makkah to Jerusalem and then on to the heavens.

Start of the Islamic movement: Rasoolullah ﷺ invited his close friends and family to Islam. Sayyiduna Ali ؓ was the cousin of Rasoolullah ﷺ and he was amongst the first to accept Islam.

The Pledge at Aqaba: In the 11th year of the mission, 6 men from Al-Madinah Al-Munawwarah pledged their allegiance to Sayyiduna Rasoolullah ﷺ.

The First Revelation: Sayyiduna Rasoolullah ﷺ received the first revelation in a cave called Hiraa. Sayyida Khadija ؓ comforted him and assured him that Allah would protect him.

The Second Pledge at Aqaba: In the 13th year of the mission, a large group of 73 men and 2 women from Al-Madinah Al-Munawwarah pledged their allegiance to Sayyiduna Rasoolullah ﷺ.

End

LESSON ONE – QURAYSH MEET AT DAR AL-NADWAH

The Evil Plot

When the Makkan Disbelievers heard about the success of Islam in Al-Madinah Al-Munawwarah, they became very worried. They were afraid that the Muslims might become very powerful one day.

In a desperate attempt to take action, 14 Makkan Chiefs met at a place called Dar Al-Nadwah. Dar Al-Nadwah was a meeting place in the city of Makkah Al-Mukarramah where the leaders of Quraysh would meet whenever an important matter needed to be discussed. As they gathered, Shaytaan also came to them disguised as a wise old sheikh who offered to advise them. He was invited to enter and joined the discussion in order to help them decide how to defeat Islam and Sayyiduna Rasoolullah ﷺ.

One of those gathered proposed that the Quraysh were no longer safe as the Muslims were gaining strength. They just had to do something in order to defeat Islam.

"We should put Muhammad ﷺ behind iron bars." said one of the Quraysh.

Shaytaan objected to this. "His followers will come and free him. You must think of a better plan." He told the leaders of Quraysh.

"Let us drive him out of Makkah!" Said another man. "We don't care what happens to him after that."

Shaytaan was not happy with this either. "His fine speech and beautiful words will make other tribes follow him. They will soon return and conquer Makkah. You must think of a better plan." He told them.

At that point, Abu Jahl, the most evil enemy of Islam, came forward with his plan. "Each clan in Makkah will provide one strong man who will come forth with a sharp sword. Then each of them will strike a blow against Muhammad ﷺ so that no single clan can be held responsible".

"This man is right!" Proclaimed Shaytaan. "It is the only thing to do."

So the leaders of Quraysh agreed that the only way to put an end to their problems was to end the life of Sayyiduna Rasoolullah ﷺ.

Allah's ﷻ Plan for Sayyiduna Rasoolullah ﷺ

Whilst the disbelievers were planning to assassinate Sayyiduna Rasoolullah ﷺ the Angel Jibreel ؏ came to him. "Do not sleep tonight in the bed on which you normally sleep" he said. Sayyiduna Jibreel also informed Sayyiduna Rasoolullah ﷺ that Allah ﷻ had granted him permission to migrate to Al-Madinah Al-Munawwarah.

> "Remember how the disbelievers plotted against you to keep you in bonds and slay you or get you out of your home. They plot and plan and Allah ﷻ plans too, but the best of planners is Allah ﷻ."
>
> وَإِذْ يَمْكُرُ بِكَ الَّذِينَ كَفَرُوا لِيُثْبِتُوكَ أَوْ يَقْتُلُوكَ أَوْ يُخْرِجُوكَ ۚ وَيَمْكُرُونَ وَيَمْكُرُ اللَّهُ ۖ وَاللَّهُ خَيْرُ الْمَاكِرِينَ
>
> Surah: Al-Anfaal, Ayah no: 30

Many of the companions of Sayyiduna Rasoolullah ﷺ had already left for Al-Madinah Al-Munawwarah. Amongst the few that remained were Sayyiduna Ali ؓ and Sayyiduna Abu Bakr ؓ.

Sayyiduna Abu Bakr ؓ had already asked Sayyiduna Rasoolullah ﷺ for permission to emigrate but it is reported that the Messenger ﷺ had told him not to hurry so much. *"It may be that Allah will grant you a companion"* said Sayyiduna Rasoolullah ﷺ according to a narration. Sayyiduna Abu Bakr ؓ had hoped that it would be the Prophet ﷺ himself.

It is reported that Sayyiduna Rasoolullah ﷺ would visit the house of Sayyiduna Abu Bakr ؓ either in the morning or at night; but on the day when he was given permission to migrate, he came to the house of Sayyiduna Abu Bakr ؓ at noon.

"Allah has given us permission to migrate." Sayyiduna Rasoolullah ﷺ told him.

"Together?" Asked Sayyiduna Abu Bakr ﷺ.

"Together" he replied.

Sayyiduna Abu Bakr ﷺ wept tears of extreme joy. He had wanted to migrate with Sayyiduna Rasoolullah ﷺ for so long and now his hopes were about to become reality.

Sayyiduna Rasoolullah ﷺ told Sayyiduna Ali ﷺ to sleep in his bed and cover himself with the mantle of Rasoolullah ﷺ. He also instructed Sayyiduna Ali to return the belongings of those who had kept them with Sayyiduna Rasoolullah ﷺ for safekeeping. Sayyiduna Ali was to meet them later in Al-Madinah Al-Munawwarah.

That night, a man from each tribe gathered around the blessed house of Sayyiduna Rasoolullah ﷺ. They were ready to commit an evil crime and try to harm the greatest of Allah's ﷻ creation.

Abu Jahl had told them what they had to do but Allah had a different plan for Sayyiduna Rasoolullah ﷺ.

EXERCISE ONE

ANSWER THE QUESTIONS BELOW.

1. Why were the chiefs of Quraysh so concerned with the success of Islam?

_____

_____

2a. Where did the 14 chiefs of Quraysh gather together to discuss how to deal with Muslims?

_____

2b. Apart from the 14 leaders of Makkah Al-Mukarramah, who else joined the meeting?

_____

3. Describe the events of the meeting and the decision that was made by the chiefs.

_____

_____

_____

_____

_____

4. Who advised our Prophet ﷺ not to sleep in the bed that he would normally sleep in?

_____

5. Who took the place of the Prophet ﷺ?

_____

6. During this period where the Meccan chiefs were plotting against the Prophet. Allah granted permission to the Prophet to migrate.

a. Where did the Prophet migrate from?

_____

b. Where did the Prophet ﷺ migrate to?

_____

c. Which of his companions accompanied him on the migration?

_____

7a. The Prophet ﷺ is known as "Al-Ameen" (Trustworthy one). What did he instruct his companion as he set off on the migration?

_____
_____

b. Why was it necessary for the Muslims to migrate? Why did they migrate to Al-Madinah Al-Munawwarah rather than any other place?

_____
_____
_____
_____
_____

LESSON TWO - THE HIJRAH

The Disbelievers had surrounded the house of Rasoolullah ﷺ poised with their sharp swords ready to assassinate him. The Angel, Sayyiduna Jibreel عليه السلام had already come to Sayyiduna Rasoolullah ﷺ and told him about their evil plan.

Sayyiduna Rasoolullah ﷺ came out of the house and blew dust in the faces of the enemy whilst reciting verses from Surah Ya Seen. Allah ﷻ blinded the Disbelievers and they were not able to see our beloved Prophet, Sayyiduna Rasoolullah ﷺ leave his house and walk away.

A while later, a man approached the Disbelievers, "Can't you see what has happened to you?" He said.

The Disbelievers put their hands on their heads and felt the dust with their hands. They immediately entered the house searching for Sayyiduna Rasoolullah ﷺ and saw a figure asleep wrapped in the blessed mantle of Rasoolullah ﷺ. When Sayyiduna Ali رضي الله عنه arose, they knew for sure that Sayyiduna Rasoolullah ﷺ had escaped. The Disbelievers were shocked to see Sayyiduna Ali رضي الله عنه and they realised that their evil plan had failed. They were not prepared to give up just yet though. They set about looking for Sayyiduna Rasoolullah ﷺ and Sayyiduna Abu Bakr رضي الله عنه. For they knew that many Muslims had left for Al-Madinah Al-Munawwarah and suspected that Sayyiduna Rasoolullah ﷺ would do the same.

A few kilometres away, Sayyiduna Rasoolullah ﷺ and Sayyiduna Abu Bakr ؓ had left Makkah Al-Mukarramah and headed towards Al-Madinah Al-Munawwarah. It is narrated that at one point, Sayyiduna Rasoolullah ﷺ halted his camel and looking back towards Makkah Al-Mukarramah said, "You are the dearest place to me on earth and the dearest to Allah. Had my people not driven me out of you I would not have left you".

By the time the Disbelievers started searching the countryside around Makkah Al-Mukarramah, Sayyiduna Rasoolullah ﷺ and his loyal companion, Sayyiduna Abu Bakr ؓ, had taken refuge in a cave in the mountain of Thoor. The leaders of Quraysh had offered a huge reward of 100 camels for anyone that could capture Sayyiduna Rasoolullah ﷺ, so many of the Disbelievers of Makkah Al-Mukarramah came out searching for him.

Sayyida Asmaa, the daughter of Sayyiduna Abu Bakr ؓ, would bring food for Sayyiduna Rasoolullah ﷺ and Sayyiduna Abu Bakr ؓ under the cover of night so that no one would be able to see where she was going. Sayyiduna Abu Bakr's ؓ son, Abdullah, would bring them news of what people in Makkah were saying so that they would know what the Disbelievers were up to.

One day, Sayyiduna Rasoolullah ﷺ and Sayyiduna Abu Bakr ؓ were still in the cave when they heard some men approaching. Their voices grew louder as they got closer and closer to the cave. Sayyiduna Abu Bakr ؓ was afraid that the enemy may find them and try to harm Sayyiduna Rasoolullah ﷺ.

It was narrated that Sayyiduna Abu Bakr ؓ said to Sayyiduna Rasoolullah ﷺ, "If one of them looks down at his feet he will see us." He said, "What do you think, O Abu Bakr, of the two with whom the third is Allah?"

Sayyiduna Rasoolullah ﷺ was under the protection of Allah ﷻ and assured Sayyiduna Abu Bakr ؓ that Allah ﷻ was with them. When the men approached the mouth of the cave, they saw that there was a spider's web and a pigeon's nest at the entrance to the cave. They agreed that they did not need to look inside the cave as no one could possibly have entered the cave without disturbing the web or the nest. Little did they realise that Allah ﷻ had sent them down to protect Sayyiduna Rasoolullah ﷺ.

After three days, Sayyiduna Rasoolullah ﷺ finally left the cave with Sayyiduna Abu Bakr. A man named Abdullah bin Arqat brought them two camels to ride on and they started to make their way towards Al-Madinah Al-Munawwarah. They were also accompanied by Aamir bin Fuhayra, who acted as their guide on the journey. They were not clear of danger yet as there were still many people hoping to attain the reward offered by the Disbelievers of Quraysh for the capture of Sayyiduna Rasoolullah ﷺ. They took a different route to the one people usually took when going to Al-Madinah Al-Munawwarah, which meant travelling along the coast by the Red sea.

It is narrated that during the journey, Sayyiduna Rasoolullah ﷺ and Sayyiduna Abu Bakr ؓ reached the house of a lady called Umm Ma'bad in an area called Qadeer. Umm Ma'bad was an old and frail woman who used to offer food and water to travellers that passed by her house. Sayyiduna Rasoolullah ﷺ wished to purchase some food from her but she had none to offer. He then noticed a weak, skinny goat near her home. It did not look as though it was strong enough to have any milk in its udders. When asked whether the goat gave any milk, Umm Ma'bad said, "No" but she gave Rasoolullah ﷺ permission to try and milk the goat. Rasoolullah ﷺ said "Bismillah" and the goat's udders were full of milk as soon as his blessed hands touched them.

After witnessing this miracle of Sayyiduna Rasoolullah ﷺ, Umm Ma'bad and her family were truly amazed and accepted Islam at the hands of the blessed prophet ﷺ Sayyiduna Rasoolullah ﷺ and Sayyiduna Abu Bakr ؓ then continued on towards their destination, the blessed city known as Yathrib which would soon come to be known as the blessed city of Al-Madinah Al-Munawwarah.

The migration of the Muslims and their beloved Messenger ﷺ had been made necessary because of the harm that they were suffering in Makkah Al-Mukarramah but Allah ﷻ provided a way out for them and opened up a new city where they could worship Allah ﷻ without suffering at the hands of Quraysh. We learn from this that protecting one's religion is so important that the Muslims sacrificed their wealth and their homes to seek a place where they could worship Allah ﷻ.

It is also important to note that even though Quraysh had refused to believe in Sayyiduna Rasoolullah ﷺ they still believed that he was a truthful and trustworthy person.

EXERCISE TWO

ANSWER THE QUESTIONS BELOW.

1. How did the Prophet ﷺ escape from the disbelievers waiting for him outside his home?

_____
_____

2. Upon leaving the city, the Prophet ﷺ and his companion took refuge in a cave, what is the name of the cave? Which mountain is the cave in?

_____

3. What was the name of the guide who accompanied them of the journey?

_____

4. When the disbelievers reached the cave that the Prophet ﷺ was taking refuge in, they did not look inside of the cave due to what they saw at the mouth of the cave. What did they see?

_____
_____

5. During the migration, the Prophet ﷺ reached the house of Umm Ma'bad in an area known as Qadeer. Describe the events that took place at the old lady's house.

_____
_____
_____
_____
_____
_____
_____
_____
_____
_____

LESSON THREE - ARRIVAL IN AL-MADINA AL-MUNAWWARAH

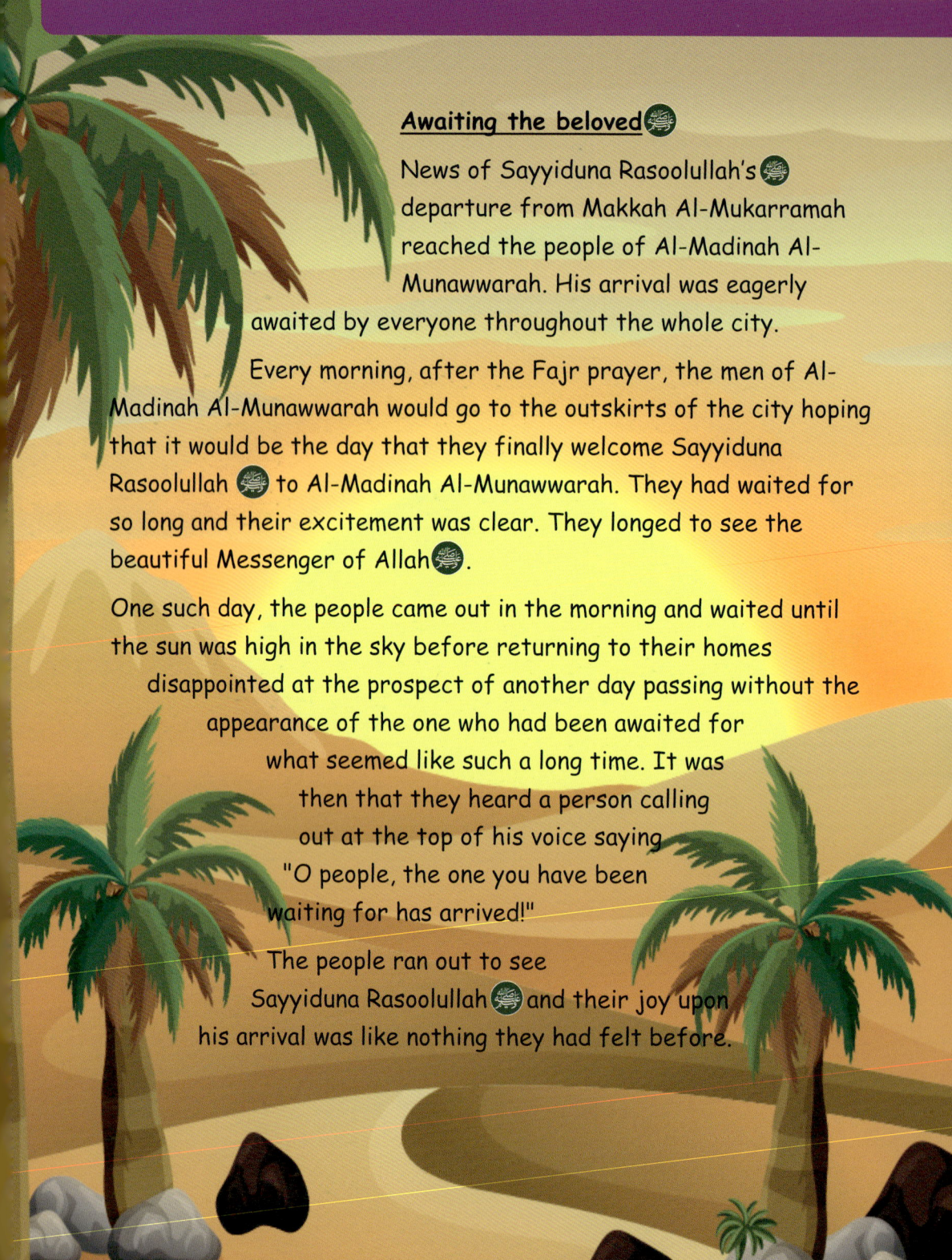

Awaiting the beloved ﷺ

News of Sayyiduna Rasoolullah's ﷺ departure from Makkah Al-Mukarramah reached the people of Al-Madinah Al-Munawwarah. His arrival was eagerly awaited by everyone throughout the whole city.

Every morning, after the Fajr prayer, the men of Al-Madinah Al-Munawwarah would go to the outskirts of the city hoping that it would be the day that they finally welcome Sayyiduna Rasoolullah ﷺ to Al-Madinah Al-Munawwarah. They had waited for so long and their excitement was clear. They longed to see the beautiful Messenger of Allah ﷺ.

One such day, the people came out in the morning and waited until the sun was high in the sky before returning to their homes disappointed at the prospect of another day passing without the appearance of the one who had been awaited for what seemed like such a long time. It was then that they heard a person calling out at the top of his voice saying, "O people, the one you have been waiting for has arrived!"

The people ran out to see Sayyiduna Rasoolullah ﷺ and their joy upon his arrival was like nothing they had felt before.

Sayyiduna Rasoolullah ﷺ and Sayyiduna Abu Bakr ؓ were of a similar age so people were not sure which of the two was the Messenger of Allah ﷻ until Sayyiduna Abu Bakr ؓ stood up to shade Sayyiduna Rasoolullah ﷺ with his own mantle. Then the people knew that they were looking at the beautiful form of Allah's ﷻ final Messenger, Muhammad ﷺ.

Sayyiduna Rasoolullah ﷺ stayed in an area called Qubaa' for a few days. Whilst he was there, he also laid the foundations of the mosque at Qubaa'. Sayyiduna Rasoolullah ﷺ would later keep a habit of visiting the mosque every Saturday. We know how blessed it is as Sahl bin Hunayf ؓ says that Rasoolullah ﷺ said: "Whoever went out until he came to this mosque, Qubaa' Mosque, and prayed therein, it would be equivalent to performing Umrah".

The Full Moon Rises

Sayyiduna Rasoolullah ﷺ and Sayyiduna Abu Bakr ؓ stayed in Qubaa' from Monday until Thursday. On Friday, the 12th of Rabi-ul-Awwal, they set off for the heart of Al-Madinah Al-Munawwarah. They offered the Friday prayer with the tribe of Banu Saalim at the bottom of a valley called Wadi Ranoonah. This was the first Jumuah prayer that Sayyiduna Rasoolullah ﷺ led in Al-Madinah Al-Munawwarah.

As they made their way towards the heart of Al-Madinah Al-Munawwarah, they passed by many people and many tribes. This was the greatest day in their lives as it was the day on which the Messenger of Allah, Sayyiduna Rasoolullah ﷺ would be joining them as an inhabitant of the blessed city.

Sayyiduna Anas ؓ, a close companion of the Prophet ﷺ said, "I was present the day he entered Al-Madinah Al-Munawwarah and I have never seen a better or brighter day than the day on which he came to us in Al-Madinah Al-Munawwarah."

The moment the people of Al-Madinah Al-Munawwarah had dreamed of had finally arrived. There was a festive atmosphere across the city as Sayyiduna Rasoolullah's ﷺ blessed camel, Qaswa, eased through the blessed streets. Everyone wanted the honour of hosting Sayyiduna Rasoolullah ﷺ. There was great joy as people thronged to see the blessed face of Sayyiduna Rasoolullah ﷺ. The joy of the people was reflected in the chants that broke out amongst the crowds.

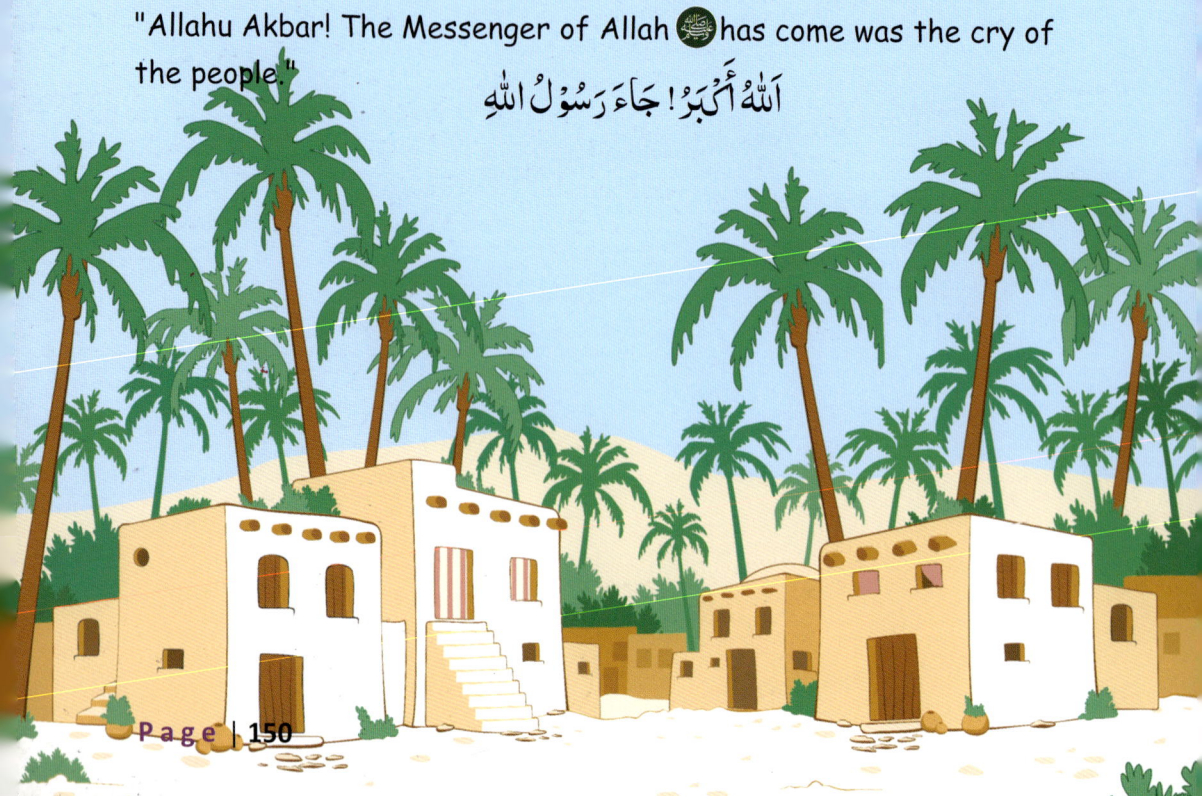

"Allahu Akbar! The Messenger of Allah ﷺ has come was the cry of the people."

اَللهُ أَكْبَرُ! جَاءَ رَسُولُ اللهِ

In the midst of the joyous scenes, some young girls from the tribes of Aws and Khazraj started to play their tambourines as they sang the famous lines:

طَلَعَ الْبَدْرُ عَلَيْنَا مِنْ ثَنِيَّاتِ الْوَدَاعِ

O the white moon rose over us
From the valley of Wadaa'

وَجَبَ الشُّكْرُ عَلَيْنَا مَا دَعَى لِله دَاعِ

So we owe it to show gratitude
Where the caller is towards Allah

أَيُّهَا الْمَبْعُوثُ فِينَا جِئْتَ بِالْأَمْرِ الْمُطَاعِ

O you who were raised amongst us
You came with the command for us to obey

جِئْتَ شَرَّفْتَ الْمَدِينَةَ مَرْحَبًا يَا خَيْرَ دَاعِ

You have brought to this city nobleness
Welcome! O best caller to God's way

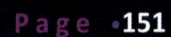

Some of the Banu Saalim came and asked him to live with them hoping that his blessed camel, whose name was Qaswa, would stop by their houses but it is reported that the Prophet ﷺ said, "Let her go her way."

Qaswa was under Allah's ﷻ command so they let her go on until she came to the homes of Banu Bayaada then moved forward to the houses of Banu Saaida and Banu Al-Haarith. Eventually, the camel came to the homes of Banu Malik and knelt at a place which was used for drying dates. It belonged to two young orphans called Sahl and Suhail. The Prophet ﷺ stayed seated on his blessed camel.

Qaswa stood up once again and walked a short distance before kneeling outside the house of a man called Khalid Ibn Zaid, who is known as Sayyiduna Abu Ayyub Al Ansari ﵁. Sayyiduna Rasoolullah ﷺ then alighted from his camel as Sayyiduna Abu Ayyub took his baggage into the house. Others invited Sayyiduna Rasoolullah ﷺ to stay with them but it is reported that he told them, "A man goes with his saddle."

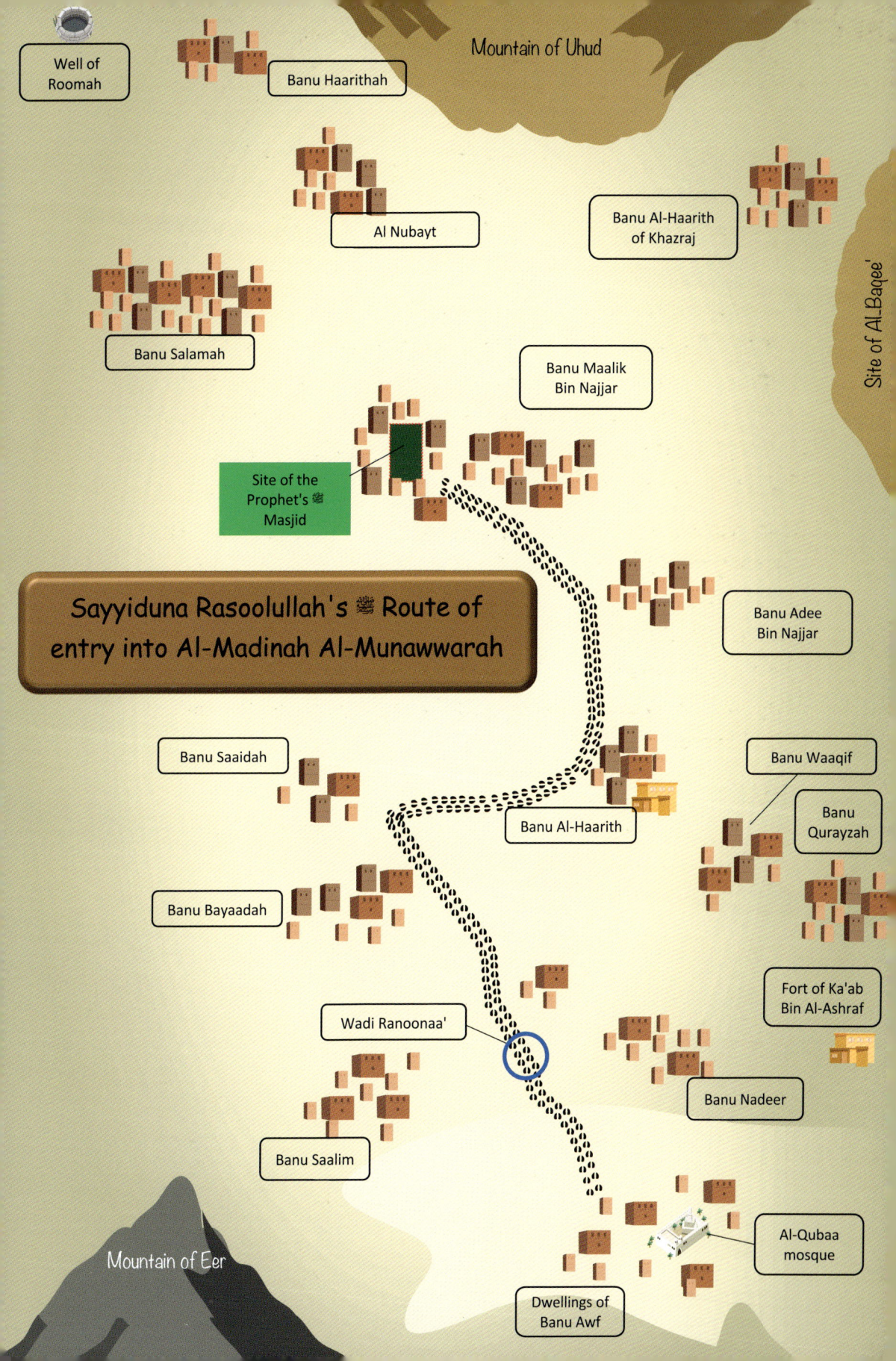

Sayyiduna Rasoolullah's ﷺ Route of entry into Al-Madinah Al-Munawwarah

- Well of Roomah
- Banu Haarithah
- Mountain of Uhud
- Al Nubayt
- Banu Al-Haarith of Khazraj
- Banu Salamah
- Site of Al Baqee'
- Banu Maalik Bin Najjar
- Site of the Prophet's ﷺ Masjid
- Banu Adee Bin Najjar
- Banu Saaidah
- Banu Waaqif
- Banu Al-Haarith
- Banu Qurayzah
- Banu Bayaadah
- Fort of Ka'ab Bin Al-Ashraf
- Wadi Ranoonaa'
- Banu Nadeer
- Banu Saalim
- Al-Qubaa mosque
- Mountain of Eer
- Dwellings of Banu Awf

EXERCISE THREE

ANSWER THE QUESTIONS BELOW.

1. Upon arrival in Al-Madinah Al-Munawwarah, where did the Prophet ﷺ stay for the first few days?

_____

2. The Prophet ﷺ laid the foundations to the mosque in Qubaa' and would visit the mosque regularly. Sahl Bin Hunayf narrates that the Prophet ﷺ said, "Whoever prays in the mosque, it would be equivalent to_____."

3. On what date did the Prophet set off from Qubaa' to the heart of Al-Madinah Al-Munawwarah?

_____

4. Qaswa the camel of the Prophet ﷺ was under the command of Allah ﷻ, she knelt down at the home of Banu Maalik on a piece of land.

a. Who did the land belong to?

_____

b. What was the land used for at the time?

_____

5. At who's house did the Prophet ﷺ reside in when he first arrived in Al-Madinah Al-Munawwarah?

_____

6. Imagine you were one of the inhabitants of Al-Madinah Al-Munawwarah who witnessed the arrival of Sayyiduna Rasoolullah ﷺ. Write a short passage explaining what you saw, heard and how you felt during that beautiful day?

_____
_____
_____
_____
_____
_____
_____
_____
_____
_____
_____
_____
_____
_____

LESSON FOUR - BUILDING OF THE MASJID

The Mosque of Rasoolullah ﷺ

Sayyiduna Rasoolullah ﷺ ordered that a mosque should be built. He wanted to purchase the land which belonged to Sahl and Suhail, the two orphans who owned the area which was used for drying dates. This was the very place where Qaswa had knelt down before arriving at the house of Sayyiduna Abu Ayyub Al-Ansari ﷺ.

Sahl and Suhail wanted to gift the land to Sayyiduna Rasoolullah ﷺ "We give it to you, O Messenger of Allah" they told him. But Sayyiduna Rasoolullah ﷺ refused to take it without payment. Sayyiduna Abu Bakr ﷺ eventually paid 10 gold coins to purchase the land from Sahl and Suhail.

Building the Prophet's ﷺ Mosque

Sayyiduna Rasoolullah ﷺ and his blessed companions set about building the mosque. Sayyiduna Rasoolullah ﷺ helped to build the mosque with his own blessed hands. The walls of the mosque were made of mud and stone. Palm trees were used as pillars in the mosque. There were also rooms built at the side of the mosque for Sayyiduna Rasoolullah ﷺ and his blessed family.

Sayyiduna Rasoolullah ﷺ gave the Muslims of Al-Madinah Al-Munawwarah the title of Ansaar, which means Helpers. The Muslims of Quraysh and other tribes who had left their homes and emigrated to Al-Madinah Al-Munawwarah were known as the Muhajiroon, meaning Emigrants.

Everyone took part in the work including Sayyiduna Rasoolullah ﷺ himself. As they worked, they chanted:

"There is no life, but the life of the next world;
Oh God, have mercy on the Ansaar and the Muhajiroon."

Building the Bonds of Brotherhood

The Muhajiroon had sacrificed many things to join Sayyiduna Rasoolullah ﷺ in Al-Madinah Al-Munawwarah. Having left their homes, families and possessions, they were in need of food and other things for themselves.

Sayyiduna Rasoolullah ﷺ gathered the Ansaar and the Muhajiroon and sought to unite the Muslims further by proposing that each person from the Ansaar takes someone from the Muhajiroon as a brother.

It is reported that Sayyiduna Rasoolullah ﷺ said, "The Muhajiroon and the Ansaar are the supporters of each other."

Sayyiduna Rasoolullah ﷺ commanded the Ansaar and the Muhajiroon to take one another as brothers. He even stood before the companions and took Sayyiduna Ali ﷜ by the hand and proclaimed,

"This is my brother."

This meant that the Muhajiroon would receive much needed help from their brothers of the Ansaar.

The Ansaar accepted the Muhajiroon as their brothers, took them into their homes and even offered them half of their own belongings. This Islamic brotherhood is known as Mu'aakhaat.

Sayyiduna Rasoolullah ﷺ taught the companions that Muslims are like one body. If one part of the body feels pain, then the whole body feels discomfort. The Muslims of Al-Madinah Al-Munawwarah helped to create a Muslim community by making sure that their brothers and sisters did not feel their pain alone.

Bringing Peace to Al-Madinah Al-Munawwarah

Al-Madinah Al-Munawwarah also had a Jewish community, which included three tribes. The Banu Nadir, the Banu Qaynuqaa and the Banu Qurayzah.

Sayyiduna Rasoolullah ﷺ wanted there to be peace amongst all people. He ﷺ made an agreement with the Jewish community that both Muslims and Jews should be free to practice their own religions whilst treating each other with respect. The Muslims and Jews of Al-Madinah would also help each other if either of them was attacked by someone. It was also agreed that the decision made by Rasoolullah ﷺ would be respected by all if there was ever to be a disagreement amongst them.

We can see how Our Prophet Muhammad ﷺ lived with other people of different faiths.

Islam helps us to live peacefully with others and we should all learn from the most beautiful example of Sayyiduna Rasoolullah ﷺ Sayyiduna Rasoolullah ﷺ had brought peace to Al-Madinah Al-Munawwarah. The city had two famous tribes. One was called Aws and the other was called Khazraj. The two tribes had fought many battles with each other but now wanted peace between the people of Al-Madinah Al-Munawwarah.

The Hypocrites

Before the arrival of Sayyiduna Rasoolullah ﷺ the people of Al-Madinah Al-Munawwarah accepted the leadership of a man named Abdullah bin Ubayy. He was a clever man who wanted to be the king of Al-Madinah Al-Munawwarah. However, his hopes had been ruined after the arrival of Sayyiduna Rasoolullah ﷺ as the people had accepted Rasoolullah's ﷺ blessed leadership.

Abdullah bin Ubayy and many of his followers hid their hatred for Sayyiduna Rasoolullah ﷺ and pretended to be Muslims. These people were dangerous enemies of Islam and started to plot ways in which they could harm Sayyiduna Rasoolullah ﷺ. These people were known as Munafiqoon (hypocrites) and were always trying to harm the Muslim.

Despite the efforts of the hypocrites to cause the Muslims harm, there was a great peace in the city for the first time. The Muslims had started fasting in Ramadaan and gathering at the mosque when the time for prayer arrived.

The Call to Prayer

People used to judge prayer times by the position of the sun in the sky but Sayyiduna Rasoolullah ﷺ wanted to summon people to the prayer.

It is narrated that one of the companions had proposed using a flag that would be raised at prayer time, others had also suggested using a horn or even a bell but this was not to be the way of the Muslims. Abdullah Ibn Zayd went away, thinking about the concern of the Messenger of Allah. He saw the Adhaan in a dream and the next morning he came to Sayyiduna Rasoolullah ﷺ and told him about it.

"O Messenger of Allah, whilst I was half-asleep, someone came to me and showed me the Adhaan."

Sayyiduna Umar Ibn al-Khattaab ؓ had also seen the dream before that but he kept quiet for twenty days. Then he told Sayyiduna Rasoolullah ﷺ who said to him, "What stopped you from telling me about it?"

"Abdullah Ibn Zayd beat me to it and I felt shy." Replied Sayyiduna Umar ؓ.

Sayyiduna Rasoolullah ﷺ addressed Sayyiduna Bilal ؓ after hearing about the dream, "O Bilal, get up and see what Abdullah Ibn Zayd tells you to do and do it." Sayyiduna Abdullah Ibn Zayd ؓ then shared the words of the Adhaan with Sayyiduna Bilal ؓ. Sayyiduna Bilal ؓ then started to make Adhaan from the tallest house in the vicinity of the mosque from that day onwards. He has been known, since that day, as the honourable Muaddhin of Rasoolullah ﷺ.

This chapter in the life of the blessed Messenger ﷺ helps to show us how important brotherhood is in Islam. Sayyiduna Rasoolullah ﷺ showed the companions how important it is to take care of our brothers and sisters in Islam by tying bonds of brotherhood between the Ansaar and Muhajiroon.

Secondly, we also learn about the importance of being true to Islam. This means acting in accordance with the commands of Allah ﷻ and His Messenger ﷺ and trying our best not to act like hypocrites.

Lastly, we can see how important it is to have a peaceful society for all human beings in Islam. Sayyiduna Rasoolullah ﷺ established peace in a city which had seen many was amongst its tribes by helping them to support and protect each other.

EXERCISE FOUR

ANSWER THE QUESTIONS BELOW.

1. Al-Masjid Al-Nabawi was built on the land purchased from the 2 orphans Sahl and Suhail.

How much was it purchased for?

1 Gold coin	5 Gold coins	10 Gold coins
50 Gold coins	100 Gold coins	1000 Gold coins

2. Who paid for the land which Al-Masjid Al-Nabawi was built on?

_____

3. Fill in the gaps

Mu'aakhat	Ansaar	Muhajiroon	Helpers	Emigrants

a. The Muslims of Al-Madinah Al-Munawwarah were given the title of _____ which means _____.

b. The people of Quraysh who came to Al-Madinah Al-Munawwarah from Makkah Al-Mukarramah were given the title of _____ which means _____.

c. Islamic brotherhood is known as _____.

4. It is reported that the Prophet ﷺ said, "The Muhajiroon and Ansaar are the supporters of each other." What lessons can we learn from this?

_____
_____
_____
_____
_____
_____

5. Al-Madinah Al-Munawwarah had a Jewish community. Name three of the tribes in the boxes below.

6. The peace and tranquillity that the Prophet ﷺ bought to Al-Madinah Al-Munawwarah through his teachings and leadership is a beautiful example for us. If you could influence society, which of the Prophet's ﷺ teachings would you apply in this day to help create peace between people.

_____
_____
_____
_____
_____
_____

LESSON FIVE - THE CUSP OF WAR

The Enmity of Quraysh

The disbelievers in Makkah Al-Mukarramah were furious that Sayyiduna Rasoolullah ﷺ had reached Al-Madinah Al-Munawwarah safely. They still wanted to harm the Muslims and they certainly did not want to let the Muslims live peacefully.

One day, a group of the Disbelievers came to Al-Madinah Al-Munawwarah and stole some camels from the blessed city. Sayyiduna Rasoolullah ﷺ ordered some people to follow them but the disbelievers escaped.

It was around this time that Allah ﷻ revealed verses that are of great importance. The Muslims had been persecuted, driven out of their homes and suffered great torture at the hands of Quraysh. They had to patiently endure the pain for years but Allah ﷻ now revealed a verse that brought many of them great joy. They had been given permission to fight against those who fought them and this gave the Muslims hope that they could defend themselves against Quraysh and anyone else that may try to harm them.

> "Permission [to fight] has been given to those who are being fought, because they were wronged. And indeed, Allah is competent to give them victory."
>
> أُذِنَ لِلَّذِينَ يُقَاتَلُونَ بِأَنَّهُمْ ظُلِمُوا وَإِنَّ اللَّهَ عَلَىٰ نَصْرِهِمْ لَقَدِيرٌ
>
> Surah: Al-Hajj, Ayah no: 39

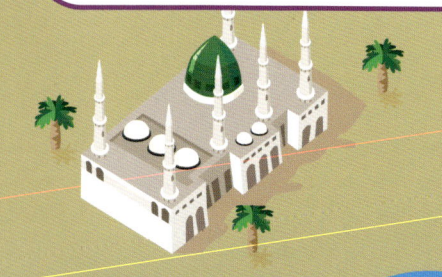

Badr

Red Sea

Abdullah Ibn Jahsh ﷺ & His Mission

In the second year after the Hijrah, Sayyiduna Rasoolullah ﷺ sent Abdullah Ibn Jahsh ﷺ on a mission with eight other Muslims. Sayyiduna Abdullah Ibn Jahsh ﷺ was also given a letter and told not to look at it until he had been travelling for two days. The letter contained a message telling him to travel to a place called Nakhla near Makkah Al-Mukarramah. Once there, they were to wait and find out whatever they could about a caravan of Quraysh that was returning to Makkah Al-Mukarramah loaded with goods. The group attacked the caravan of the Quraysh and ended up taking their goods.

Sayyiduna Abdullah Ibn Jahsh ﷺ returned to Al-Madinah Al-Munawwarah safely having taken two people from the caravan as prisoners along with their goods. Sayyiduna Rasoolullah ﷺ did not approve of their actions and knew that the Disbelievers would want to take revenge. "I did not order you to fight in the sacred month" He told them.

That same year, during the month of Ramadaan, a leader of Quraysh by the name of Abu Sufyan was returning from Syria with a large caravan containing money and merchandise accompanied by more than thirty men. Abu Sufyan feared that he would be caught by the Muslims so he sent a man named Dumdum Ibn Amr to Makkah Al-Mukarramah so that he could call upon men from Quraysh to protect the caravan.

The Muslim Army Rises

The Makkans swiftly sent an army of 1000 men out towards Al-Madina Al-Munawwarah. When Sayyiduna Rasoolullah ﷺ heard the news that the disbelievers of Makkah Al-Mukarramah had left with 1000 men he consulted with his companions. "Give me advice, O men" he said to them.

One of the great companions of Sayyiduna Rasoolullah ﷺ was a man named Sa'ad Ibn Mu'adh ﷺ. He stood up and said, "We are with you and by Allah ﷻ if you were to ask us to cross this sea and you plunged into it then we would plunge into it with you." Sayyiduna Rasoolullah ﷺ was delighted when he heard the words of Sa'ad Ibn Mu'adh ﷺ. He commanded the Muslims to get ready so that they could defend Islam. They left Al-Madinah Al-Munawwarah with just 313 men, 70 camels, 3 horses and a few swords.

The Muslim army was heading to a place called Badr near Al-Madinah Al-Munawwarah. It was an open plain and a number of wells were to be found there. Sayyiduna Rasoolullah ﷺ knew the importance of water in the usually hot and dry climate of Arabia and he wanted to ensure that the Muslims had the opportunity to secure water for themselves. He ﷺ led the army forward to ensure that they reached the plains of Badr in time to secure access to a well. When the Muslim army reached the first well they came to and stopped, a man named Hubaab Ibn Al-Mundhir came to Sayyiduna Rasoolullah ﷺ with an idea.

"Take us on, O Messenger of Allah," He said, "Until we come to one of the large wells which is nearest to the enemy. Let us halt there and block the wells beyond it and make a cistern for ourselves. Then we will fight the enemy and all the water will be ours."

The Muslims knew that Sayyiduna Hubaab﷌ had a brilliant plan and they made sure that they followed it. A cistern was built, every man filled his water container and some of the wells were blocked so that Quraysh could not access water.

Sayyiduna Rasoolullah ﷺ supplicated to Allah ﷻ and it is reported that He ﷺ said, "O Allah! If this small group of believers is to perish this day, then there will be no one left on earth to worship you and carry your message forward to the world.

The Battle Commences

The Muslim army met the army of the Disbelievers of Quraysh and the battle took place on Friday the 17th of Ramadaan. The Muslim army was much smaller than that of the disbelievers of Quraysh but Allah ﷻ sent angels to help the Muslims so that they would win the battle.

"Be of good cheer O Abu Bakr!" Sayyiduna Rasoolullah ﷺ told His greatest companion Sayyiduna Abu Bakr ﷌, "Here is Jibreel and in his hand is the rein of a horse which he is leading, and he is armed for war."

Three of the Quraysh stepped forward intending to start the battle. Utbah, Shaybah and Walid were the first to challenge the Muslims to open combat. It is reported that Sayyiduna Rasoolullah ﷺ eventually turned to three men of his own family to answer their challenge. It is reported that Sayyiduna Rasoolullah ﷺ then called out;

"Arise O Ubaydah!" Calling out a man from his own extended family named Ubaydah Ibn Al-Harith. He had accepted Islam in Makkah Al-Mukarramah and was now at the forefront of the Muslim army.

The Battlefield of Badr

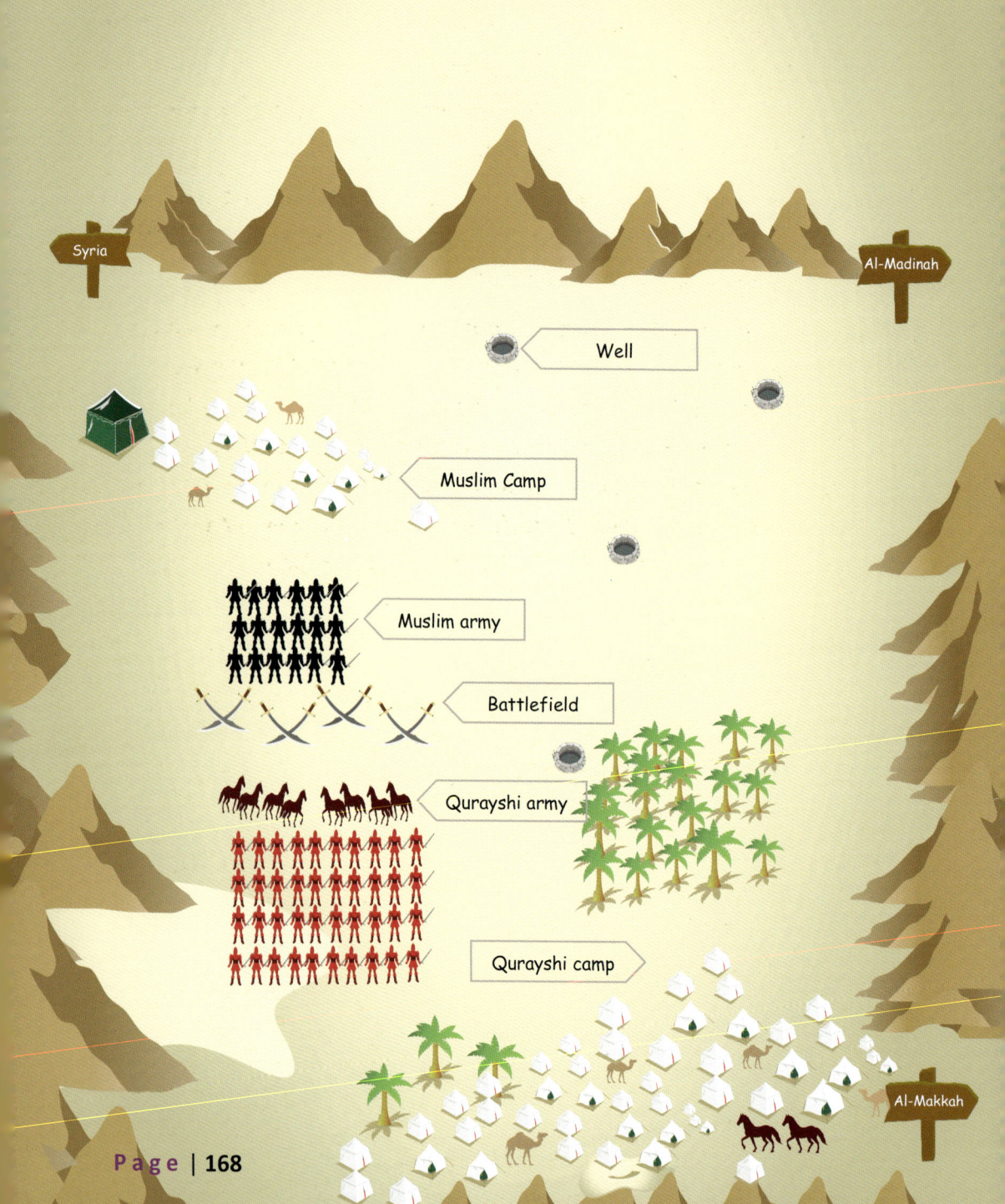

Syria

Al-Madinah

Well

Muslim Camp

Muslim army

Battlefield

Qurayshi army

Qurayshi camp

Al-Makkah

"Arise O Hamzah!" He said, calling upon his beloved uncle Hamzah, who was known as the Lion of Allah ﷻ. For he was a strong and fearsome fighter.

"Arise O Ali!" Called Allah's Messenger ﷺ, turning to Sayyiduna Ali ﺭﺿﻲ ﺍﻟﻠﻪ ﻋﻨﻪ who was not only the Prophet's ﷺ cousin but had also lived with Sayyiduna Rasoolullah ﷺ in Makkah Al-Mukarramah. Ali ﺭﺿﻲ ﺍﻟﻠﻪ ﻋﻨﻪ was still a young man and he was full of courage.

Utbah, Shaybah and Walid were soundly beaten by the Muslim fighters. In the midst of the battle though, Sayyiduna Ubaydah ﺭﺿﻲ ﺍﻟﻠﻪ ﻋﻨﻪ was mortally wounded and lost part of his leg.

Soon, the battle was in full flow as both armies fought. In the midst of battle, Sayyiduna Ukkasha ﺭﺿﻲ ﺍﻟﻠﻪ ﻋﻨﻪ, one of those special companions in the army, found that his sword had broken. It is reported that he went to Sayyiduna Rasoolullah ﷺ who gave him a wooden club. Sayyiduna Ukkasha ﺭﺿﻲ ﺍﻟﻠﻪ ﻋﻨﻪ took it and as he held it in his hand it became a gleaming, long, strong sword. He fought with it in many battles and the sword was known as Al-Awn which means Divine Help.

Allah Helps The Believers With An Army of Angels

The Muslim army charged at their enemy but they were not alone. Allah's help was with them and an army of Angels charged with them. They came over an area known as the mountain of Angels and soon the Quraysh were soundly defeated by the Muslim army at Badr. The victory was a miracle as they had been so badly outnumbered by Quraysh but Allah had taught the Muslims an important lesson. When Allah helps people then none can overcome them except by Allah's will.

Seventy of the disbelievers were killed including some of the greatest enemies of Islam such as Shaybah, Umayyah Ibn Khalaf and the evil Abu Jahl. As many as seventy of the disbelievers were taken back to Al-Madina Al-Munawwarah as prisoners. The disbelievers returned to Makkah Al-Mukarramah defeated and disheartened but they were determined to take revenge for the deaths of their leaders.

The battle of Badr strengthened the Muslims and soon the whole of Arabia heard about their amazing victory. After the battle, Allah revealed a Surah about the battle. The Surah is called Al-Anfaal.

EXERCISE FIVE

ANSWER THE QUESTIONS BELOW.

1. Why did the Disbelievers of Quraysh send out an army towards Al-Madinah Al-Munawwarah?

_____
_____
_____
_____

2. How many men were in each of the two armies?

_____
_____

3. What did Sayyiduna Rasoolullah ﷺ do when he heard about the enemy approaching Al-Madinah Al-Munawwarah?

_____
_____
_____
_____
_____

4. Why was it important for Sayyiduna Rasoolullah ﷺ to consult his blessed companions before going to fight the army of the disbelievers from Quraysh?

_____
_____
_____
_____
_____

5. Describe what happened in the battle of Badr. Why was victory so important for the Muslims? What lessons did you learn from the battle of Badr?

_____
_____
_____
_____
_____
_____
_____
_____
_____

مَا تَعُدُّونَ أَهْلَ بَدْرٍ فِيكُمْ قَالَ مِنْ أَفْضَلِ الْمُسْلِمِينَ ـ أَوْ كَلِمَةً نَحْوَهَا ـ قَالَ وَكَذَلِكَ مَنْ شَهِدَ بَدْرًا مِنَ الْمَلَائِكَةِ

Sayyiduna Jibreel ﷺ came to the Prophet ﷺ and said, "How do you look upon the warriors of Badr among yourselves?" The Prophet ﷺ said, "As the best of the Muslims." or said a similar statement. On that, Sayyiduna Jibreel ﷺ said, "And so are the Angels who participated in the Badr (battle)."

LESSON SIX - BATTLE OF UHUD

After losing the battle at Badr, the Disbelievers of Quraysh were ashamed at the way in which they had been beaten and wanted to take revenge against the Muslims.

The Quraysh started to gather a large army to attack the Muslims again and they had some 3000 soldiers ready to fight just one year after the battle of Badr.

Sayyiduna Rasoolullah ﷺ Consults His Companions

Meanwhile, in Al-Madinah Al-Munawwarah, Sayyiduna Rasoolullah ﷺ consulted his blessed companions and asked them whether they wanted to fight the Quraysh outside of Al-Madinah Al-Munawwarah or whether they preferred to defend Al-Madinah Al-Munawwarah from within the city.

Many of the young companions of the Prophet ﷺ had not been at the battle of Badr and they wanted to go out of the city. They tried to convince Sayyiduna Rasoolullah ﷺ to agree with them. Many of the elder companions wanted to stay within the city and this was also the wish of Sayyiduna Rasoolullah ﷺ. He eventually decided to go with the view of the young companions and put on his armour for battle. The young companions, having realised that Sayyiduna Rasoolullah ﷺ preferred to stay within the city, regretted what they had said but Sayyiduna Rasoolullah ﷺ had already put his armour on.

"It is not fitting that a Prophet who has put on his armour should lay it aside until he has fought" said the blessed Messenger ﷺ.

The Hypocrites Desert The Muslims

Sayyiduna Rasoolullah ﷺ then set off with a thousand men until they reached a place called Al-Shaut between Al-Madinah Al-Munawwarah and Uhud. Amongst the Muslim army there were a number of hypocrites. Their leader was a man named Abdullah Ibn Ubayy and he started to tell his friends and followers to return back to the city. He complained about the fact that the blessed Messenger ﷺ Sayyiduna Rasoolullah ﷺ had listened to what the young companions had said when they were asked about whether the Muslim army should go out of the city or not. Abdullah Ibn Ubayy then turned back along with some 300 hypocrites.

The Muslim army was reduced to just 700 men to fight against the 3000 strong army of Quraysh. This was a difficult test for the Muslims but Sayyiduna Rasoolullah ﷺ bravely moved on to Uhud and the army marched until they were between the mountain of Uhud and the army of Quraysh.

The Muslims Fight With Valour

Sayyiduna Rasoolullah ﷺ placed some 50 of the best archers on a hill and told them not to leave their position no matter what happened in the battle.

"Keep the cavalry away from us with your arrows and do not let them come on us from the rear whether the battle goes in our favour or against us: and keep your place so that we cannot be targeted from your direction" ordered our Prophet ﷺ.

Sayyiduna Rasoolullah ﷺ now brandished a sword and asked, "Who will take this sword, together with its right?" Immediately, Sayyiduna Umar Ibn Al-Khattaab ؓ came forward to take it but Sayyiduna Rasoolullah ﷺ turned away from him and again asked, "Who will take this sword, together with its right?" Another companion by the name of Zubayr, wearing a yellow turban that stood out amongst those on the battle field, said he would take it but again Allah's Messenger ﷺ turned away repeating the question a third time.

"What is its right, O Messenger of Allah?" Said a companion known as Abu Dujanah ؓ.

"Its right is that you should strike the enemy with it until its blade is bent."

"I will take it, together with its right," replied Abu Dujanah.

Sayyiduna Abu Dujanah ؓ, whose real name was Simaak ibn Kharashah, was one of the great warriors amongst the Muslim ranks. He wore a red turban on the battlefield and was known for being an excellent Swordsman.

Once the battle started, he fought with the special sword given to him by Sayyiduna Rasoolullah ﷺ. He fought with so much courage that he overcame anyone who came up to fight against him.

Another special fighter was someone truly loved by Sayyiduna Rasoolullah ﷺ. Sayyiduna Hamzah ﷺ was one of the Prophet's ﷺ uncles and he was known as the "Lion of Allah". Like Abu Dujanah ﷺ, he fought with amazing courage and killed many of the Quraysh's fighters. As Sayyiduna Hamzah ﷺ was battling the Quraysh, a man named Wahshi was watching him from a distance. Wahshi used a spear to strike Sayyiduna Hamzah ﷺ from behind. Sayyiduna Hamzah ﷺ died from the wound and his death would bring great sadness to Sayyiduna Rasoolullah ﷺ.

The Archers' Dilemma

The Muslims were rampant and chased the army of Quraysh further and further away from where the battle had started. As the fighters of Quraysh started to flee, some of the Muslims thought that the fighting was over. They ran out to try and take some of the belongings left behind by the Quraysh. Even some of the Archers, who had been told to stay in their places, moved away from their positions. Their leader, Sayyiduna Abdullah Ibn Jubayr ﷺ, tried to remind them of Sayyiduna Rasoolullah's ﷺ order to remain in their positions no matter what happened but they replied that the Prophet ﷺ had not meant for them to stay there forever.

Khalid Ibn Al-Waleed was one of the leaders of Quraysh who was leading their cavalry. He saw that the archers had moved from their position and realised that it was a chance to attack the Muslims. He marched forward with a group of soldiers and approaching from behind them, attacked and overcame the archers who had stayed in their positions. They were then able to attack the Muslims from behind and the fighters of Quraysh, who had been running away from the battle, were now returning to the battle field emboldened by Khalid Ibn Al-Waleed's response. Ikrimah, another of the Quraysh's cavalry leaders, followed Khalid Ibn Al-Waleed in doing the same.

Quraysh Seize Their Opportunity

The Muslims were now faced with great difficulty as Quraysh attacked them. Sayyiduna Rasoolullah ﷺ was also struck by a stone. One of his blessed teeth was damaged and his blessed lip was also injured. There were a only small number of companions who fought to protect Sayyiduna Rasoolullah ﷺ.

Almost all of the companions protecting Sayyiduna Rasoolullah ﷺ were killed until there was just one man known as Ziyad left. Suddenly, a number of the Muslims returned to protect Sayyiduna Rasoolullah ﷺ. Abu Dujanah ؓ courageously made his body a shield for Sayyiduna Rasoolullah ﷺ and there were a number of arrows that struck him and got stuck in his back. Another companion named Anas Ibn Nadr ؓ was later found with more than 80 wounds on his body which he received defending Sayyiduna Rasoolullah ﷺ.

The beloved Messenger ﷺ was then struck on his blessed helmet by a man of Quraysh known as Ibn Qamiah. Two of the spikes from the helmet broke off and sunk into his blessed cheek. One of the companions named Abu Ubaydah Ibn Al-Jarrah ؓ pulled the spikes out with his own teeth to help Sayyiduna Rasoolullah ﷺ. The companions could not tolerate any kind of discomfort when it came to the honour of Sayyiduna Rasoolullah ﷺ and it was clear that they would gladly give their lives to defend him.

The Muslims, many of whom had left the battle earlier, eventually returned and they all gathered at a nearby mountain where they could take shelter.

Abu Sufyaan was a leader of the Quraysh and after the battle ended he went to the top of a mountain and shouted, "Victory in war goes in turns. Today is in revenge for Badr". He then started shouting, "May Hubal rise!" which was a war cry that Quraysh made in calling for help from their false God.

Sayyiduna Rasoolullah ﷺ commanded Sayyiduna Umar ؓ to stand up and answer Abu Sufyaan by saying, *"Allah is most high and most glorious. We are not equal. Our dead are in paradise and your dead are in hell."*

The Aftermath

The Muslims came onto the battlefield to search for their martyrs. What they found made them very sad indeed. Quraysh had cut the noses and ears of some of the martyred Muslims. Sayyiduna Hamza ؓ, the uncle of Sayyiduna Rasoolullah ﷺ, even had his stomach cut open. This was truly painful for Sayyiduna Rasoolullah ﷺ and he shed tears when he saw his beloved uncle.

Sayyiduna Rasoolullah ﷺ then brought the martyrs together and prayed over them before burying them. Some 70 Muslims were martyred in the battle of Uhud and to this day Muslims visit their graves when they travel to Al-Madinah Al-Munawwarah.

The battle of Uhud holds many important lessons for us as Muslims. Firstly, it shows that Muslims will do anything to protect the honour of their Prophet, Sayyiduna Muhammad ﷺ. It also shows us the importance of obeying Sayyiduna Rasoolullah ﷺ. All success lies in obeying Allah ﷻ and His Messenger ﷺ and the story of the battle of Uhud teaches us how important this is.

All success lies in obeying Allah ﷻ and His Messenger ﷺ and the story of the battle of Uhud teaches us that success lies only in obeying Allah ﷻ and Sayyiduna Rasoolullah ﷺ.

We also learned how important it is to consult others before doing something important from the actions of Sayyiduna Rasoolullah ﷺ before the battle of Uhud.

The Battle of Uhud Illustrated

The Muslim army lines up to face disbelievers of Quraysh at Uhud.

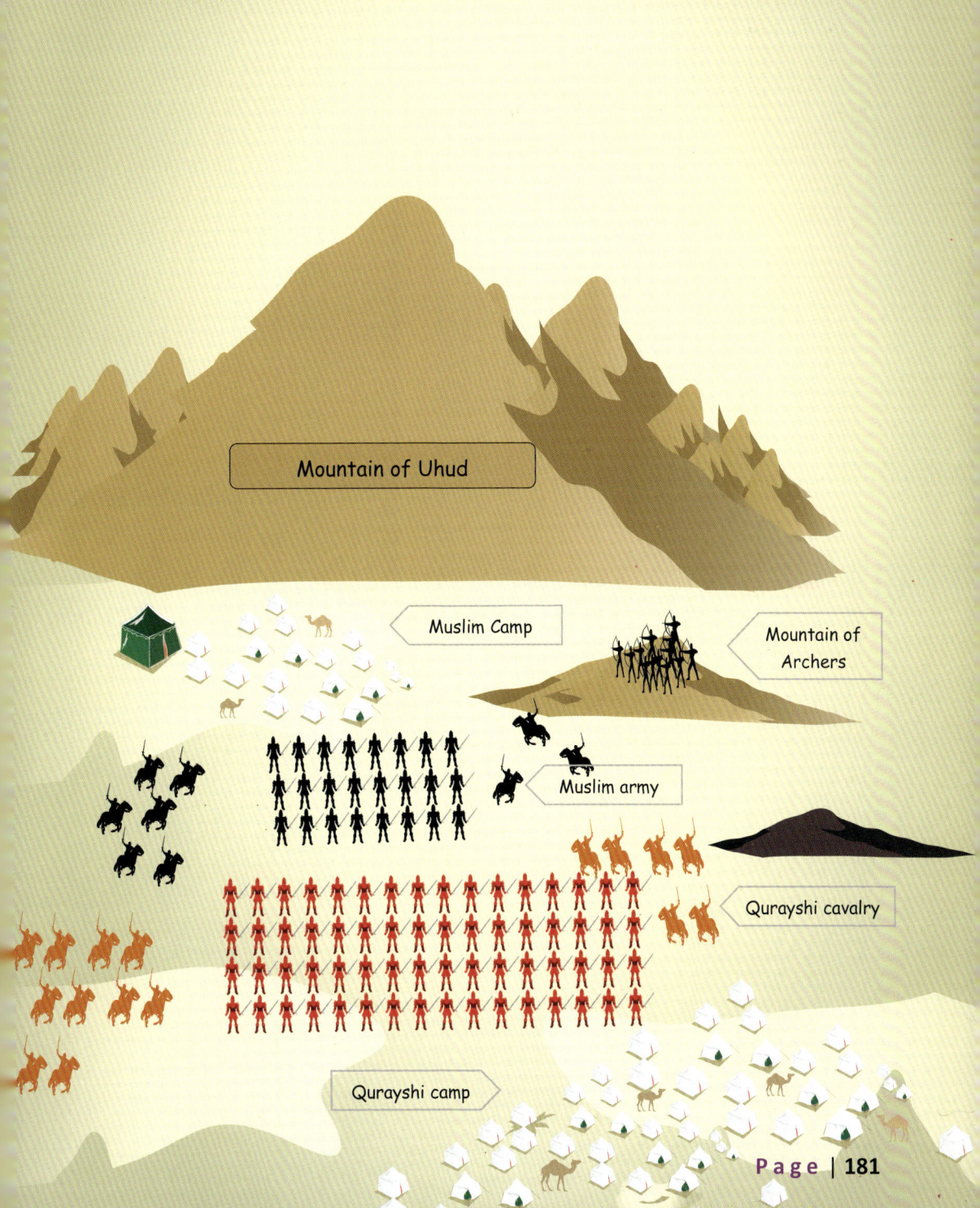

Mountain of Uhud

Muslim Camp

Mountain of Archers

Muslim army

Qurayshi cavalry

Qurayshi camp

The Muslim army are rampant and force the Quraysh to retreat further and further back. Some of the archers move away from their positions believing that victory was certain.

Khalid Ibn Al-Waleed sees that the Archers have moved out of position and takes the opportunity to attack the Archers from the rear.

The Qurayshi cavalry overcomes the Archers and attacks the Muslims from the rear. The Qurayshi fighters return to the heart of the battle and force the Muslims to retreat.

EXERCISE SIX

ANSWER THE QUESTIONS BELOW.

1. What were the two options that Sayyiduna Rasoolullah ﷺ had in order to defend the city?

_____

_____

2. What did the hypocrites do on the way to Uhud? What reason did they give for doing so?

_____

_____

_____

_____

_____

3. What did Sayyiduna Rasoolullah ﷺ do with the Archers? What did he order them not to do?

_____

_____

_____

_____

4. Describe what happened during the battle of Uhud and explain what you have learned from the battle.

HADITH: THE VIRTUES OF UHUD

عَنْ أَنَسِ بْنِ مَالِكٍ ـ رضى الله عنه أَنَّ رَسُولَ اللَّهِ صلى الله عليه وسلم طَلَعَ لَهُ أُحُدٌ فَقَالَ "هَذَا جَبَلٌ يُحِبُّنَا وَنُحِبُّهُ، اللَّهُمَّ إِنَّ إِبْرَاهِيمَ حَرَّمَ مَكَّةَ، وَإِنِّي أُحَرِّمُ مَا بَيْنَ لاَبَتَيْهَا

Narrated Anas bin Malik ﷺ:

When the mountain of Uhud came in the sight of Allah's Messenger ﷺ he said. "This is a mountain that loves us and we love it. O Allah! Ibrahim ﷺ made Makkah a sanctuary, and I make (the area) in between these two mountains (of Al-Madinah) a sanctuary."

LESSON SEVEN - BATTLE OF AL-AHZAAB

When Sayyiduna Rasoolullah ﷺ first arrived in Al-Madinah Al-Munawwarah, the Jewish tribes had agreed to help the Muslims defend the city whilst living in peace.

Some of the Jewish tribes failed to keep their promise as part of the agreement and had tried to harm the Muslims. Sayyiduna Rasoolullah ﷺ responded by leading the Muslim army to their fort and laying siege to it. After more than two weeks, the Banu Qaynuqa surrendered and then left Al-Madinah Al-Munawwara before settling in Syria.

The Banu Nadir had also betrayed the Muslims and had tried to poison Sayyiduna Rasoolullah ﷺ whilst he was on a visit to one of their houses. The Muslims also laid siege to the Banu Nadir before they also surrendered and left Al-Madinah Al-Munawwarah taking their many valuables with them on hundreds of camels.

The Alliance

The Quraysh were still intent on destroying the Muslims and they had been working hard to gather a large army since returning from the battle of Uhud. A man from the Jewish tribe of Banu Nadir called Huyay Ibn Akhtab came to Makkah Al-Mukarramah and agreed an alliance with Quraysh to try and destroy the Muslims. They agreed that Quraysh would march out from Makkah Al-Mukarramah and join up with the Jewish tribes as well as others who had some enmity towards the people of Al-Madinah Al-Munawwarah.

In the fifth year after the Hijrah, Quraysh set out from Makkah with 4000 men and marched towards Al-Madinah Al-Munawwarah. A group of horsemen from the tribe of Banu Khuzaa'ah set out from Makkah Al-Mukarramah at speed to warn Sayyiduna Rasoolullah ﷺ about the emerging army. The Muslims had one week to prepare for war. Sayyiduna Rasoolullah ﷺ called his companions to discuss how to win against such a large army. One of the companions, who was known as Salman Al-Farsi ؓ, stood up and said:

"O Messenger of Allah, in Persia, when we feared an attack from people riding horses, we would surround ourselves with a trench. So let us dig a trench around ourselves now."

Everyone agreed to this plan. The Muslims set about digging a trench which the armies of Quraysh and their allies would not be able to cross. Sayyiduna Rasoolullah ﷺ and his companions would work on the trench from dawn until dusk. Sayyiduna Baraa' ؓ was a companion of the Prophet ﷺ and like so many others, he was struck by the beauty of the scene he saw before him. He watched for a moment as the Muslims were working hard to complete the trench.

He was amazed by the beauty of the Messenger of Allah ﷺ and would later say, "More beautiful than him I have not seen."

Overcoming Adversity

Digging the trench was no easy task and the companions faced many challenges. In the midst of difficulty, the Companions would turn to Sayyiduna Rasoolullah ﷺ and on one such occasion, Sayyiduna Umar ﷺ went to the Prophet ﷺ to complain of a rock they could not break. Sayyiduna Rasoolullah ﷺ took the pick axe from him and gave the rock a blow which created a flash of lightning over the city towards the South. He then struck another blow and this time there was a flash towards Uhud in the North. The third blow split the rock into pieces and this time the light flashed eastwards.

Sayyiduna Salman ﷺ asked Sayyiduna Rasoolullah ﷺ about the flashes.

"Did you see them Salman? By the light of the first I saw the castles of Yemen; by the light of the second I saw the castles of Syria; by the light of the third I saw the white palace of Khosrow."

"Through the first, Allah opened up Yemen to me; through the second He has opened up Syria and the West for me; and through the third the East"

The companions took great joy in being close to Sayyiduna Rasoolullah ﷺ even though this was not always an easy time for the Muslims. They did not have much food and one of the companions, who went by the name of Abu Talha ﷺ, complained to the Prophet ﷺ about their hunger, showing him a stone that he had tied to his stomach to make the pain of hunger easier to bear.

The Prophet ﷺ revealed his own blessed stomach and all were surprised to see that he had tied not one but two stones to his stomach.

The Arrival of The Enemy

The Quraysh and their allies arrived with a huge army just as the Muslims had finished digging the trench. It had taken the Muslims about six days to complete it and the enemy were surprised by what they found before them. The trench formed a barrier between them and Al-Madinah Al-Munawwarah whilst the Muslim army was some three thousand strong and ready to defend the city.

The Quraysh and their alles tried to find narrow spots along the trench which would be easier to cross over but when they did so the Muslims were ready to push them back. They then lay siege to Al-Madinah Al-Munawwarah whilst attacking the Muslims with arrows and spears. The Quraysh realised that they needed to weaken the Muslim army so that their numbers at the trench would be reduced but they had to find a way in which some of the Muslim army could be moved away from the trench.

The conditions were still difficult for the Muslims and things were made worse when Banu Qurayzah, one of the Jewish tribes who had agreed to help the Muslims in defending the city, betrayed the Muslims and decided to join the Quraysh in attacking the Muslims. Word of their treachery soon reached Sayyiduna Rasoolullah ﷺ and many of the hypocrites who were amongst the Muslim army started to make excuses and soon returned to their homes claiming they were worried about their women and children.

Very soon after this, a man from the enemy's army, Naeem Bin Mas'ood, sneaked across the trench and came to Sayyiduna Rasoolullah ﷺ. He had accepted Islam in secret so the enemy did not know that he was Muslim and asked the Prophet ﷺ how he could help at this difficult time. He left with a very clever plan.

He went to the Bani Qurayzah, who were about to join the Quraysh to fight against the Muslims. Naeem ؓ told them that the Quraysh were going to leave the battle and that they would not help Bani Qurayzah after this, which would leave the tribe of Bani Qurayzah alone to face the Muslims. Naeem ؓ also told the Quraysh that Bani Qurayzah were secretly plotting to take some of the leaders of Quraysh and hand them over to the Muslims so Quraysh should not trust Bani Qurayzah either.

Naeem used the same clever trick with Ghatafan and some other tribes. The tribes invading Al-Madinah Al-Munawwarah were now doubting their trust in each other.

The Quraysh and their allies had now laid siege to the city for almost 20 days and the Muslims were exhausted. This was a test of their faith in Allah ﷻ. Sayyiduna Rasoolullah ﷺ continued to pray to Allah ﷻ for help and one night, Allah ﷻ sent strong winds which blew the tents of Quraysh and the allies away.

Having been unable to break down the Muslim defences, the invading armies had run out of patience. Abu Sufyan, the leader of the Qurayshi army, made his way back to Makkah with the men of Quraysh. Soon after that, the Ghatafan tribe also left and the Muslims found that all the enemy forces had left by the next morning.

The Muslims praised Allah ﷻ. Thanking him for granting them a miraculous victory and saving them from defeat. This is mentioned in the Qur'an when Allah ﷻ said:

"O people who believe! Remember the favour of Allah upon you when some armies came against you, so we sent against them a windstorm and the armies you could not see; and Allah sees your deeds."

The Muslims lived under the fear of the invading armies for more than a month and had become weak due to a lack of food. Allah ﷻ tested the Muslims who had to remain patient even though they faced so much fear and hardship.

We must never forget the great sacrifices that Sayyiduna Rasoolullah ﷺ and the great companions made for Islam. This is why the Messenger of Allah ﷺ is the most beloved person to us in all creation.

The battle of the trench teaches us how important it is to be patient in order to gain success. The Muslims showed great patience and trust in Allah ﷻ before Allah ﷻ granted them victory.

Sayyiduna Rasoolullah ﷺ took part in digging the trench with his own blessed hands. This shows us how important it is for everyone to work together in order to achieve important goals for Islam.

Another beautiful lesson is that whenever the companions came across a problem, they would turn to Sayyiduna Rasoolullah ﷺ for help. They knew that the Messenger of Allah ﷺ brought them the truth from Allah and they loved him dearly for the overflowing beauty he brought. Whenever they turned to Sayyiduna Rasoolullah ﷺ their problems would be solved. Likewise, Muslims must remember that turning to Sayyiduna Rasoolullah ﷺ by following his every command will aid us in bringing about success.

Sayyiduna Rasoolullah ﷺ and the blessed companions went through so much pain and difficulty to establish Islam. We must never forget their sacrifices and all that they did for us. This is also why we love the Prophet ﷺ and his companions so dearly.

The Battle of Al-Ahzaab

- Quraysh
- Ghatafaan
- Kinaanah
- Bani Sulaym
- Bani Asad

Muslim Army

Muslim Camp

The Prophet's ﷺ mosque

Khazraj

Al-Baqee

Khazraj

Banu Nadeer

Banu Qurayzah

Qubaa'

Page | 195

EXERCISE SEVEN

ANSWER THE QUESTIONS BELOW.

1. Who failed to keep to the agreement to defend Al-Madinah Al-Munawwarah and who tried to poison Sayyiduna Rasoolullah ﷺ?

_____

_____

2. Who came up with the idea to dig a trench? Why was it so useful? Where did he learn how to use a trench in war?

_____

_____

3. What happened when Sayyiduna Umar ؓ complained to Rasoolullah ﷺ about the rock? What does this mean?

_____

_____

_____

_____

_____

_____

_____

4. Which tribes joined Quraysh in trying to defeat the Muslims? Why do you think they joined the Quraysh and not the Muslims?

_____
_____
_____
_____
_____
_____
_____

5. How were the Muslims given victory in the battle?

_____
_____
_____
_____
_____
_____
_____
_____

6. What did you learn from the battle?

_____
_____
_____
_____

LESSON EIGHT - RASOOLULLAH'S ﷺ BLESSED LINEAGE

Sayyiduna Rasoolullah ﷺ is the most respected in Allah's ﷻ creation. Here we will look at his blessed lineage and learn about the names of his blessed forefathers.

He is our Master Muhammed the Messenger of Allah ﷺ, the son of <u>Abdullah</u>, the son of <u>Abdul Muttalib</u>, the son of <u>Hashim</u>, son of <u>Abd Manaf</u>, son of <u>Qusayy</u>, son of <u>Kilaab</u>, son of <u>Murra</u>, son of <u>Ka'b</u>, son of <u>Lu'ayy</u>, son of <u>Ghaalib</u>, son of <u>Fihr</u>, son of <u>Maalik</u>, son of <u>Nadr</u>, son of <u>Kinaana</u>, son of <u>Khuzayma</u>, son of <u>Mudrika</u>, son of <u>Ilyas</u>, son of <u>Mudar</u>, son of <u>Nizaar</u>, son of <u>Ma'add</u> the son of <u>Adnan</u>.

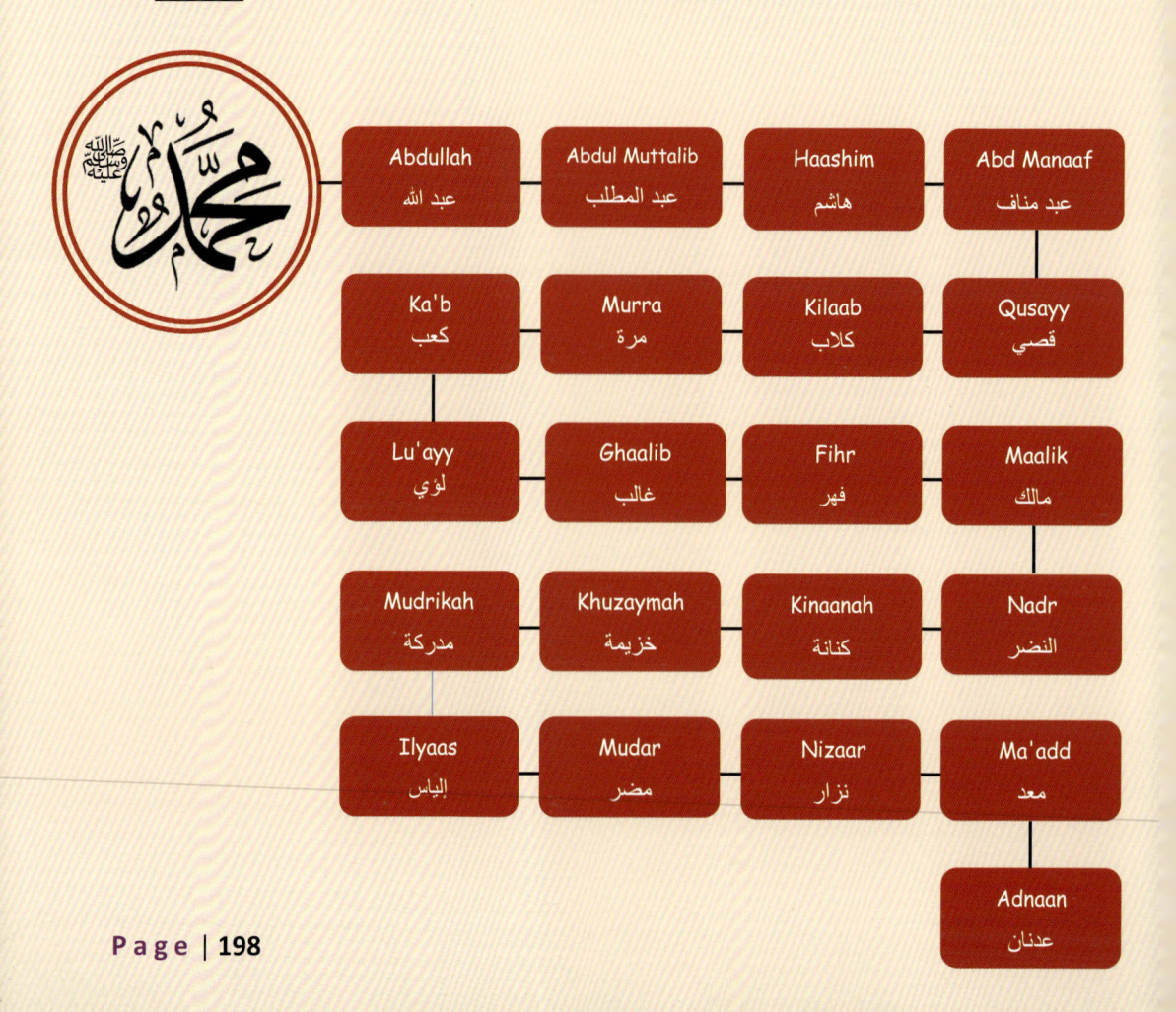

محمد ﷺ	Abdullah عبد الله	Abdul Muttalib عبد المطلب	Haashim هاشم	Abd Manaaf عبد مناف
	Ka'b كعب	Murra مرة	Kilaab كلاب	Qusayy قصي
	Lu'ayy لؤي	Ghaalib غالب	Fihr فهر	Maalik مالك
	Mudrikah مدركة	Khuzaymah خزيمة	Kinaanah كنانة	Nadr النضر
	Ilyaas إلياس	Mudar مضر	Nizaar نزار	Ma'add معد
				Adnaan عدنان

EXERCISE EIGHT

MEMORISE THE BLESSED LINEAGE OF RASOOLULLAH ﷺ.

Memorise the lineage of Sayyiduna Rasoolullah ﷺ and ensure you can prove to your teacher that you have memorised it.

Once you have recited the blessed lineage of Sayyiduna Rasoolullah ﷺ, your teacher will sign this box.

LESSON NINE - THE BEAUTY OF HIS ﷺ BLESSED FORM

Allah ﷻ created Sayyiduna Rasoolullah ﷺ in a form that will not be matched by anyone else. He is the most beautiful person to ever have been created.

Sayyiduna Jaabir ؓ was once with the Prophet ﷺ on the night when the full moon was shining in the sky. Sayyiduna Jaabir ؓ said, "I once saw Rasoolullah on the night of a full moon. On that night, he wore red clothes. At times, I looked at the full moon and at times I looked at Rasoolullah. In the end, I realised that Rasoolullah was more handsome, beautiful and radiant than the full moon."

Sayyiduna Rasoolullah ﷺ was neither really tall nor really short.

His skin was neither extremely pale nor dark brown.

His blessed hair was extremely black and neither extremely curly or lank.

Sayyiduna Rasoolullah ﷺ was of medium stature with broad shoulders and a full head of hair that reached down to his earlobes.

His blessed head was large and so were his joints.

His blessed face was slightly round in shape. It shone like the light of the full moon.

His blessed complexion was radiant and had a tinge of redness.

His eyes were wide and his pupils were very black whilst his eyelashes were beautifully lush.

When he walked, he walked with vigour, it was as though he was walking down a slope.

The messenger of Allah ﷺ was light. When he would walk in sunlight or moonlight he did not cast a shadow.

The seal of Prophecy was found between his blessed shoulders.

He had a slight space between his eyebrows.

Sayyiduna Rasoolullah ﷺ was the finest and most beautiful of people.

The palms of the Prophet's ﷺ hands were softer than silk, and his scent was like that of the hand of a perfumer, whether he applied scent or not. When he would shake someone's hands, that person would smell the Prophet's ﷺ scent upon him for the remainder of his day. And when the Prophet ﷺ would pat the head of a young child, that young child would stand out among all other children due to the scent of his head.

BELONGINGS OF RASOOLULLAH

As far as Rasoolullah ﷺ was concerned about his maintenance, he was content with as much as he needed and abstained from anything more than that. He would wear a cloak (Rida'), a course garment, or a thick outer garment.

The most beloved article of clothing that the messenger of Allah ﷺ wore was the shirt (Qamis). The sleeve of his shirt would reach his wrist. When he would wear a shirt, he would begin with the right side.

The Messenger of Allah ﷺ owned a pair of pants (Saraaweel) and he wore a pair of sandals known as (Taasuma).

Ibn Abbas ؓ related, "The Messenger of Allah said, Wear white clothing. Let your living wear them and use them to shroud your dead, for indeed white is the best of your clothing."

The Messenger of Allah ﷺ would wear a white Qalansuwa. A Qalansuwa is a cap. He would wear a Qalansuwa under his turban. He would wear white Yemeni Qalansuwas that had stuffing inside of them. When the Prophet ﷺ would tie his turban he would let its tail hang between his shoulders.

The ring of Rasoolullah ﷺ was silver and its stone was Abyssinian. He would take the stone of his ring and turn it inwards toward his palm. The engraving on his ring was such that one line had *Muhammad*, the line above it had *Rasool*, and the line above it had *Allah* ﷻ.

The Prophet's ﷺ sword was of Hanafi make. It is called Hanafi because it was made by the Banu Hanifa tribe, who were well known for their excellence in sword making. The Prophet ﷺ had numerous swords. They include: Al-Qadeeb, Al-Qalai, Al-Battar, Al-Hatf, Al-Mikhdham, Al-Rasub, Al Samsaama, Al-Lahif, Dhu Al-Fiqar.

The Prophet ﷺ had a helmet made of iron called Al-Muwashah – which was adorned with copper and another helmet, called As-Sabugh, or Dhu As-Sabugh.

The name of camel was Qaswa. The name of his Mule was Duldul. The name of his donkey was Ya'fur

Some of the Horses of Rasoolullah ﷺ were: Sakb, Murtajiz, Lahif, Lizaz, Zarib, Ward, Sab'hah, Ya'sub

EXERCISE NINE

FILL IN THE GAPS BELOW.

1. Write a poem in praise of Sayyiduna Rasoolullah ﷺ. It does not have to rhyme but make sure you try and mention as much praise of Sayyiduna Rasoolullah ﷺ as you can. Your poem should be no less than 8 lines.

_____
_____
_____
_____
_____
_____
_____
_____

2. Make a poster about the blessed belongings of Rasoolullah ﷺ. Ensure it is colourful and use it to help others learn about them. Use a separate piece of paper.

Qamar Learning Academy

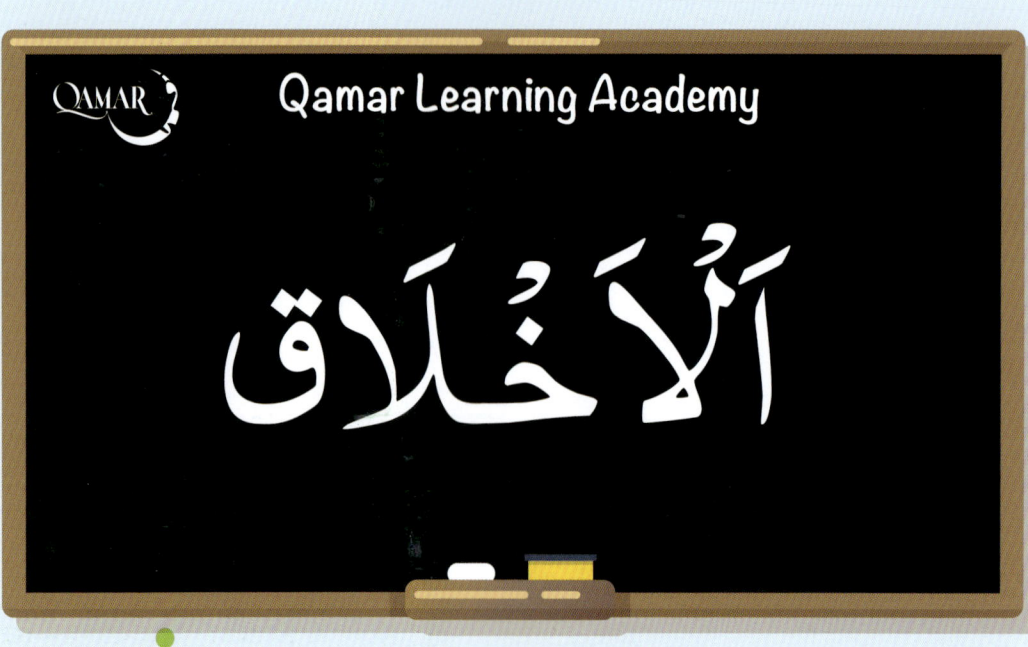

اَلْاَخْلَاق

What's in this section?

DHIKR (REMEMBRANCE) OF ALLAH

KINDNESS TO PARENTS
- Etiquettes of a good relationship with parents
- Relations with parents after their death

BACKBITING
- How to avoid backbiting

JEALOUSY

PRIDE

VISITING THE SICK
- Manners of visiting the sick

HALAL AND HARAAM FOODS
- Things that are Halal to consume
- Ingredients

AKHLAQ

LESSON ONE - DHIKR (REMEMBRANCE) OF ALLAH ﷻ

WHEN YOU REMEMBER ALLAH ﷻ, HE REMEMBERS YOU. ALLAH ﷻ SAYS IN A HADITH QUDSEE, "*I AM AS MY SERVANT THINKS I AM, AND I AM WITH HIM WHEN HE REMEMBERS ME. IF HE MAKES MENTION OF ME TO HIMSELF, I MAKE MENTION OF HIM TO MYSELF. AND IF HE MAKES MENTION OF ME IN A GATHERING, I MAKE MENTION OF HIM IN A GATHERING BETTER THAN IT.*"

يَقُولُ اللَّهُ تَعَالَى: أَنَا عِنْدَ ظَنِّ عَبْدِي بِي، وَأَنَا مَعَهُ إِذَا ذَكَرَنِي، فَإِنْ ذَكَرَنِي فِي نَفْسِهِ، ذَكَرْتُهُ فِي نَفْسِي، وَإِنْ ذَكَرَنِي فِي مَلَإٍ، ذَكَرْتُهُ فِي مَلَإٍ خَيْرٍ مِنْهُمْ

Dhikr of Allah ﷻ is truly amazing. The beloved Messenger of Allah ﷺ would always remember Allah ﷻ before going to bed, upon waking up, before entering the toilet, upon leaving it, upon entering and leaving the mosque, before and after eating and drinking, in the morning and in the evening and at all other times.

Benefits of making Dhikr of Allah ﷻ:

- It drives away Shaytaan.
- It is pleasing to Allah ﷻ.
- It removes the worries of the heart and brings happiness to it.
- It illuminates the face and the heart.
- It saves one from Allah's ﷻ punishment.
- It erases sins.
- It is a good way to help avoid backbiting, lies and vain talk.

NOTE: Each specific form of Ibadah such as Salah, Sawm and Hajj are all different acts of Dhikr.

There are many ways to perform the Dhikr of Allah ﷻ. They include the following:

- Recite the Qur'aan as this is one of the best forms of Dhikr.

- **The Prophet** ﷺ said, "There are 2 statements which are light on the tongue, heavy upon the scale of deeds and are loved by the Most Merciful ﷻ.

> كَلِمَتَانِ خَفِيفَتَانِ عَلَى اللِّسَانِ ثَقِيلَتَانِ فِي الْمِيزَانِ حَبِيبَتَانِ إِلَى الرَّحْمَنِ
> سُبْحَانَ اللَّهِ وَبِحَمْدِهِ سُبْحَانَ اللَّهِ الْعَظِيمِ
>
> "Glory be to Allah, His is the praise, Glory be to Allah, the Most Great."

- Abu Musa ؓ said, "The Messenger of Allah ﷺ said to me "Shall I not direct you to one of the treasures of Paradise?" I said, "Yes Messenger of Allah." He said: "La Hawla Wa La Quwwata Illa Billah"

> لاَ حَوْلَ وَلاَ قُوَّةَ إِلاَّ بِاللَّهِ
>
> "There is neither power nor might except through Allah."

● Abu Hurairah ﷺ narrated that the Messenger of Allah ﷺ said, "Whoever recites:

> سُبْحَانَ اللَّهِ وَبِحَمْدِهِ
>
> "Glory be to Allah, His is the praise"

100 times a day, Allah ﷻ will forgive all his sins even if they are like the foam of the sea." (Al-Bukhari)

● The Messenger of Allah ﷺ said, "He who utters 10 times:

> لَا إِلَهَ إِلَّا اللَّهُ وَحْدَهُ لَا شَرِيكَ لَهُ، لَهُ الْمُلْكُ وَلَهُ الْحَمْدُ وَهُوَ عَلَى كُلِّ شَيْءٍ قَدِيرٌ
>
> "There is no god but Allah alone, He has no partner, His is the kingdom and His is the praise and He is capable over everything."

He will have a reward equal to that for freeing four slaves from the offspring of Ismail." (Al-Bukhari)

EXERCISE ONE

1. Select and memorise one of the Dhikrs we have mentioned in the previous chapter and recite it to your teacher.
   - Set a time and place at home to perform this Dhikr. Make a note of how much time you spend performing the Dhikr and count how many times you recite the Dhikr.
   - Teach the Dhikr you have memorised to members of your family and to your friends. Count how many people you have shared this with.

2. Design a poster describing in your own words how you felt whilst performing the Dhikr.

LESSON TWO - KINDNESS TO PARENTS

OUR PARENTS ARE A SPECIAL GIFT TO US FROM ALLAH ﷻ. THEY RAISE US MAKING MANY SACRIFICES AND UNDERGOING GREAT DIFFICULTIES. OUR ENTRY INTO JANNAH WILL DEPEND ON HOW WE HAVE TREATED OUR PARENTS. WE THEREFORE NEED TO BE GRATEFUL, RESPECTFUL AND OBEDIENT TO THEM. IF WE LOOK AT OUR PARENTS WITH MERCY AND LOVE, WE GET THE REWARD OF AN ACCEPTED HAJJ.

Allah ﷻ says in the Holy Qur'aan, "And we have enjoined on man to be good and dutiful to his parents."

وَوَصَّيْنَا الْإِنسَانَ بِوَالِدَيْهِ حُسْنًا

(Surah: Al-Ankabut, Ayah no: 8)

Sayyiduna Abdullah bin Umar ؓ narrated that the Prophet ﷺ said, "The pleasure of your Lord lies in the pleasure of your parents and the displeasure of your Lord lies in the displeasure of your parents."

رِضَا الرَّبِّ فِي رِضَا الْوَالِدِ، وَسَخَطُ الرَّبِّ فِي سَخَطِ الْوَالِدِ

The supplication of three people is always accepted; one who is oppressed, a traveller and a father for his son.

ثَلَاثُ دَعَوَاتٍ مُسْتَجَابَةٌ لَا شَكَّ فِيهِنَّ دَعْوَةُ الْمَظْلُومِ وَدَعْوَةُ الْمُسَافِرِ وَدَعْوَةُ الْوَالِدِ عَلَى وَلَدِهِ

Asma' bint Abu Bakr As-Siddiq ؓ said, "My mother came to me and she was still an idol worshipper (disbeliever), so I asked the Messenger of Allah ﷺ, "My Mother dislikes Islam and has come to visit me. Shall I be kind to her?" He replied, "Yes, be kind to your mother." (Al-Bukhari)

ETIQUETTES OF A GOOD RELATIONSHIP WITH PARENTS

- Parents should be treated well as they are a means of blessings in both worlds.

- Parents should be thanked for the love and affection with which they raised you.

- Parents should always be kept happy.

- Parents should be looked after when they are old and you should seek their forgiveness.

- Listen to parents' views as they are more experienced.

- Be humble and modest in the presence of your parents.

- Parents should be considered the owners of all your wealth and possessions.

- You should spend your wealth and time on your parents generously with an open and happy heart.

- Parents should always be appreciated and never raise your voice to them.

- Love your parents and pray for them.

RELATIONS WITH PARENTS AFTER THEIR DEATH

Abu Usayd Malik Ibn Rabi'ah narrated that a companion asked the Prophet ﷺ, "Is there any kindness that I can do to my parents after their death? The Prophet ﷺ replied, "Yes you can:

- Invoke blessings on them;
- To continue to supplicate (dua) for their forgiveness;
- To carry out the final instructions in their will;
- To keep good relations with their family and honour their friends."

يَا رَسُولَ اللَّهِ هَلْ بَقِيَ مِنْ بِرِّ أَبَوَيَّ شَىْءٌ أَبَرُّهُمَا بِهِ بَعْدَ مَوْتِهِمَا قَالَ نَعَمِ الصَّلَاةُ عَلَيْهِمَا وَالِاسْتِغْفَارُ لَهُمَا وَإِنْفَاذُ عَهْدِهِمَا مِنْ بَعْدِهِمَا وَصِلَةُ الرَّحِمِ الَّتِي لَا تُوصَلُ إِلَّا بِهِمَا وَإِكْرَامُ صَدِيقِهِمَا

Abu Dawud

This narration explains that good relations with parents is something that does not end when they pass away. We should always remember this and act upon these orders.

EXERCISE TWO

1. Design a leaflet or an instruction book showing how to be kind to parents and why. Include in this at least two Hadiths about being kind to parents. Present it to your teacher.

LESSON THREE - BACKBITING

BACKBITING IS TO SAY SOMETHING ABOUT SOMEONE THAT THEY MAY DISLIKE EVEN IF IT IS TRUE. IT IS A NASTY HABIT AND HURTS THE OTHER PERSON. TO GOSSIP AND SPREAD RUMOURS ABOUT A PERSON IS ALSO BACKBITING. IT CAUSES HATRED AND IS A MAJOR SIN.

Allah ﷻ says in Holy Qur'aan, *"And backbite not one another. Would one of you like to eat the flesh of his dead brother? You would hate it (so hate backbiting). And fear Allah. Verily, Allah is the One Who forgives and accepts repentance, Most Merciful."* (Surah Al-Hujurat, Ayah no: 12)

يَا أَيُّهَا الَّذِينَ آمَنُوا اجْتَنِبُوا كَثِيرًا مِّنَ الظَّنِّ إِنَّ بَعْضَ الظَّنِّ إِثْمٌ وَلَا تَجَسَّسُوا وَلَا يَغْتَب بَّعْضُكُم بَعْضًا أَيُحِبُّ أَحَدُكُمْ أَن يَأْكُلَ لَحْمَ أَخِيهِ مَيْتًا فَكَرِهْتُمُوهُ وَاتَّقُوا اللَّهَ إِنَّ اللَّهَ تَوَّابٌ رَّحِيمٌ

Abu Hurairah ؓ reported, The Prophet ﷺ said, *"He who believes in Allah and the Last Day must either speak good or remain silent."*

وَمَنْ كَانَ يُؤْمِنُ بِاللهِ وَالْيَوْمِ الآخِرِ، فَلْيَقُلْ خَيْراً أَوْ لِيَصْمُتْ

Al-Bukhari

Some of the reasons why people backbite are:
- Anger towards another person.
- They think of themselves as better than others.
- Jealousy towards another person.
- Disagreement about something.

HOW TO AVOID BACKBITING

KEEP IN MIND THE SERIOUSNESS OF COMMITTING THE SIN.

BE CONSCIOUS THAT ALLAH KNOWS EVERYTHING THAT WE THINK AND DO.

ADMIRE THE GOOD QUALITIES OF A PERSON, RATHER THAN BEING CRITICAL OF THEIR WEAKNESSES.

IF WE ARE AMONGST FRIENDS WHO ARE BACKBITING THEN DISCOURAGE SUCH DISCUSSIONS BY:

1. CHANGING THE TOPIC
2. CORRECTING THEM IN A PLEASANT MANNER
3. WALKING AWAY

IT IS IMPORTANT THAT WE REMEMBER TO ALWAYS BE HONEST. WE MUST ALWAYS SAY ONLY THAT WHICH IS NECESSARY. AFTER ALL, OUR RELIGION TEACHES US TO HAVE A GOOD RELATIONSHIP WITH EVERYONE, MUSLIMS AND NON-MUSLIMS.

EXERCISE THREE

ANSWER THE FOLLOWING QUESTIONS.

1. Define the term backbiting and describe what may be considered as backbiting.

   _____
   _____
   _____

2. What does Allah ﷻ say in the Qur'aan about those who backbite?

   _____
   _____
   _____

3. Identify some of the reasons that may lead a person to backbite.

   _____
   _____
   _____
   _____

4. Explain how backbiting can be avoided.

_____
_____
_____
_____
_____
_____
_____

5. Ahmed once used foul language. Many months later, Ridwaan mentioned this to his friends and told them that he thinks Ahmed is a bad person.

a. Is this backbiting?

Explain your answer.

_____
_____
_____
_____
_____

b. Ridwaan believes that this is not backbiting because what he said was true. Do you agree? Explain your answer.

_____
_____
_____
_____
_____
_____

LESSON FOUR - JEALOUSY

JEALOUSY IS TO BE DISPLEASED AT THE GOOD FORTUNE OF ANOTHER PERSON AND TO DESIRE THAT THE PERSON IS DEPRIVED OF THAT. JEALOUSY IS A DISEASE OF THE HEART AND CAN AFFECT OUR THINKING AND BEHAVIOUR.

إِيَّاكُمْ وَالظَّنَّ فَإِنَّ الظَّنَّ أَكْذَبُ الْحَدِيثِ وَلَا تَجَسَّسُوا وَلَا تَحَسَّسُوا وَلَا تَنَافَسُوا وَلَا تَحَاسَدُوا وَلَا تَبَاغَضُوا وَلَا تَدَابَرُوا وَكُونُوا عِبَادَ اللَّهِ إِخْوَانًا

Abu Hurairah ﷺ narrated that The Prophet ﷺ said, "Beware of suspicion, for suspicion is the worst of false tales; and do not look for the others' faults and do not spy, and do not be jealous of one another, and do not desert (cut your relationship with) one another, and do not hate one another; and O Allah's worshippers, be brothers (as Allah has ordered you!")."

Al-Bukhari

It has been narrated that Our Prophet ﷺ once mentioned that there was a man who had Jannah destined for him. Abdullah Ibn Umar ﷺ followed this person so that he could learn his actions. Upon witnessing nothing extraordinary, he quizzed the man only to hear the man reply, "I do not have any grudge or envy in my heart against any Muslim for that goodness which Allah has blessed him with."

Shaytaan was destroyed because of his jealousy over Adam. A jealous person will suffer themselves before any harm reaches the victim. Amongst the harm that comes to one who is jealous we find:

- Sadness which will remain forever.
- Difficulties for which no reward shall be gained.
- Allah ﷻ is displeased with a jealous person.
- Jealousy destroys a person's life and good deeds.

EXERCISE FOUR

1. Find and read the story about Prophet Yusuf ﷺ about how his brothers were jealous of him. After you have read it, write your own story about jealousy.

   You can write your story in the space provided or in a format which you prefer.

LESSON FIVE - PRIDE

PRIDE IS WHEN A PERSON THINKS THEY ARE BETTER THAN OTHERS. THE ARABIC TERM FOR PRIDE IS TAKABBUR. ALLAH SAYS IN THE HOLY QUR'AAN, *"AND DO NOT TURN YOUR FACE AWAY FROM MEN, WITH PRIDE, NOR WALK IN INSOLENCE (DISRESPECT) THROUGH THE EARTH; FOR ALLAH DOES NOT LOVE A PROUD BOASTER."*

وَلَا تُصَعِّرْ خَدَّكَ لِلنَّاسِ وَلَا تَمْشِ فِي الْأَرْضِ مَرَحًا إِنَّ اللَّهَ لَا يُحِبُّ كُلَّ مُخْتَالٍ فَخُورٍ

Our Prophet said, "None shall enter Paradise who has in his heart the weight of a mustard seed of pride."

وَلَا يَدْخُلُ الْجَنَّةَ أَحَدٌ فِي قَلْبِهِ مِثْقَالُ حَبَّةِ خَرْدَلٍ مِنْ كِبْرِيَاءَ

A proud person can be identified through the following signs:

- They refuse to apologise when they are wrong.
- They will not like a poor person to sit next to them because they look down on them.
- They will not attend gatherings hosted by poor friends or relatives.
- They hesitate to greet people because they think them to be lower than themselves.

Pride is thinking...
- She is not as clever as me.
- I am better looking than her.
- I am wealthy and she is poor.

EXERCISE FIVE

ANSWER THE FOLLOWING QUESTIONS.

1. Define the term Pride and describe what may be considered as Pride.
   _____
   _____

2. Explain some of the reasons that would make a person feel proud.
   _____
   _____
   _____
   _____

3. Explain how you could avoid pride in your life and give reasons as to why you think this would work.
   _____
   _____
   _____
   _____
   _____
   _____
   _____
   _____

LESSON SIX - VISITING THE SICK

VISITING THE SICK IS A GREAT ACT AND SUNNAH OF OUR BELOVED PROPHET MUHAMMAD ﷺ. THE PROPHET ﷺ WOULD GO AND VISIT THE SICK, HE WOULD SUPPLICATE FOR THEM AND WOULD OFFER WORDS OF SUPPORT AND ENCOURAGEMENT TO THEM.

When a relative, friend, neighbour or anyone who is known to us falls ill, we should visit them. This is an act which pleases Allah ﷻ

Abu Musa Al-Ash'ari ؓ reported that the Prophet ﷺ said, *"Feed the hungry, visit the sick and set free the captives."*

أَطْعِمُوا الْجَائِعَ، وَعُودُوا الْمَرِيضَ، وَفُكُّوا الْعَانِيَ

Al-Bukhari

Sayyiduna Abu Hurairah ؓ reported that the Prophet ﷺ said, *"Whenever a person goes to visit a sick person, a caller calls out from heaven and supplicates for them, 'May you be happy, may your walking be blessed and may you obtain a great status in paradise.'"*

مَنْ عَادَ مَرِيضًا نَادَى مُنَادٍ مِنَ السَّمَاءِ طِبْتَ وَطَابَ مَمْشَاكَ وَتَبَوَّأْتَ مِنَ الْجَنَّةِ مَنْزِلًا

Ibn Majah

MANNERS OF VISITING THE SICK

When visiting the sick, one should begin by greeting him and then asking about his health.

One should look at the sick during the visit.

One should not talk negatively whilst in the presence of the sick or their family.

Give encouragement and provide reassurance to the sick and their family that Allah willing they will be cured soon.

Do not speak in a loud tone or cause excessive noise whilst in the presence of the sick.

Even if you don't know the sick person, you must still express compassion and sympathy.

If the sick person says something unpleasant or insulting, do not take it to heart.

Request the sick to make dua for yourself as the dua of a sick person is like the dua of the angels. However, if the sick is in severe difficulty or pain, then you should not.

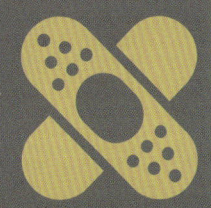

One should not visit the sick for a long period.

LESSON SEVEN - HALAL & HARAAM FOODS

There are various types of food and drink that Allah ﷻ allows us to consume. These are called Halal food and drink. Allah ﷻ wants us to eat and drink those things which are Halal. Halal food is good for our health.

It is not allowed for a Muslim to eat or drink anything which is not Halal. If a Muslim eats or drinks something which is not Halal, that person's Duaa may not be accepted.

Things that are Haraam to consume:

- Pig.
- Animals which hunt for their food such as lions, dogs, cats etc.
- Dead animals and birds.
- Animals slaughtered without mentioning the name of Allah ﷻ.
- Gelatine which is from a Haraam animal.
- Alcohol such as wine.

Things that are Halal to consume:

If any animals besides those mentioned above are slaughtered by mentioning the name of Allah ﷻ, they will be Halal to eat. Some examples are:

- Goat.
- Sheep.
- Cow.
- Chicken.

It is permissible to eat all types of fish. They do not need to be slaughtered by mentioning the name of Allah ﷻ.

It is important that we check the ingredients in foods and drinks we buy from the shops as some may contain Haraam ingredients such as:

- Alcohol
- Animal fats
- Gelatine (commonly found in sweets)
- E471 – An ingredient that is sometimes made from animal fats.

As Muslims, we should carefully choose which takeaways we buy our fast food from. Meat products such as burgers served in many takeaways may be Haraam, therefore we must refrain from eating from such places and look for places which are Halal.

NOTE: Many products have the sign "Suitable for vegetarians" on them, this does not mean that product is Halal to consume as it may have alcohol in it. Therefore, always check the ingredients before buying.

EXERCISE EIGHT

1. Think of 5 different foods. Research their ingredients and state whether they are Halal or Haraam.

If you find any food which is Haraam, list the ingredient(s) that makes it Haraam.

Food Item	Halal/Haraam	Any Haraam Ingredients
Sunny Chocolate Bar	Haraam	Pork Gelatine